A Critical Guide to Tolstoy's *On Life*

A peer-reviewed publication of
Tolstoy Studies Journal (*TSJ*) and
the Tolstoy Society of North America

Dedication

James Scanlan (1927–2016), Ohio State Emeritus, was our friend, mentor, and teacher and a lifelong inspiration for the study of Russian philosophy and intellectual history. Jim disputed Tolstoy's theodicy ardently, and ardently wanted to see this book in print. He passed away as the volume's essays were being formatted.

Robert Whittaker (1940–2016), of Lehman College, City University of New York, will be gratefully remembered as one of the pioneers of archival cooperation between American and Russian scholars. His work in making archival research relevant and alive in the digital age will remain a model.

We dedicate this volume to their memory.

A Critical Guide to Tolstoy's *On Life*
Interpretive Essays

edited by Inessa Medzhibovskaya

General Editor
Michael A. Denner

TOLSTOY STUDIES JOURNAL
DeLand, FL & Toronto, Canada

A Critical Guide to Tolstoy's *On Life*.
Interpretive Essays/Inessa Medzhibovskaya, Editor

Copyright © 2019 by the Tolstoy Society of North America

Michael A. Denner, General Editor
SPREES @ Stetson University
DeLand, FL 32724
tolstoy-studies-journal.com

Tolstoy Studies Journal is a peer-reviewed publication supported by the College of Arts and Sciences and Stetson's Program in Russian, East European, and Eurasian Studies. It receives additional assistance from the Centre for Russian and East European Studies and the Department of Slavic Languages and Literatures of the University of Toronto.

ISBN - 9781097167609
Library of Congress Control Number:2019905487

Table of Contents

Editor's Acknowledgments

During a roundtable at the American Association for the Advancement of Slavic Studies in November 2010 in Los Angeles, before the contours of this volume were finalized, we contributors explored various ideas with Randall Poole, Michael Denner, Michael Gordin, Jeff Love, and Jim Scanlan. We benefited very much from the discussion during the session, were encouraged by general interest in *On Life* and by the roundtable's high attendance, and received further recommendations and feedback. Eugene Thacker, my colleague at the New School, who is one of the most inspired interpreters of life and pessimism working today, joined us on an optimistic note in 2013. I am grateful to all the contributors to this volume for their incredible faith that a whole volume on one of Tolstoy's most controversial philosophical essays has the right to be, and that the most deserving venue for it will be found, and also for their unflagging, steadfast support and collegiality.

Very special thanks to the *Tolstoy Studies Journal*, the Tolstoy Society of North America, and especially Michael A. Denner. Michael, you never doubted that this book would see the light of day and provided all the intellectual, moral, logistical, and technical support for this to happen. Heartfelt gratitude to our readers and commentators. To Donna Orwin, President of the Tolstoy Society of North America, who is always a source of inspiration and support. To Caryl Emerson for her valuable advice. To Olga Knizhnik and Joel de Lara of the Philosophy Department at the New School, thank you for everything. And to Susan Veach, our book and production designer, who is simply the best.

This volume complements Leo Tolstoy, *On Life: A Critical Edition*, edited by Inessa Medzhibovskaya, translated by Michael Denner and Inessa Medzhibovskaya (Evanston, IL: Northwestern University Press, published in November, 2018) and my monograph volume *Tolstoy's On Life (from the Archival History of Russian Philosophy)* forthcoming from the same imprint of the Tolstoy Society of North America, 2019. I am grateful to Trevor Perri and Anne Gendler of Northwestern University Press for many helpful suggestions about how all these books could be coordinated and organized.

We shall hereafter abbreviate Leo Tolstoy, *On Life: A Critical Edition* as *OLCE*, *Tolstoy's On Life (from the Archival History of Russian Philosophy)* as *OLAH*, and this volume as *CG*.

Inessa Medzhibovskaya

Abbreviations

GV:

Николай Яковлевич Грот в очерках, воспоминаниях и письмах товарищей и учеников, друзей и почитателей. Санкт-Петербург: Типография Министерства Путей Сообщения, 1911

ИРЛИ РАН:

Институт Русской Литературы Российской Академии Наук (also PD, Пушкинский Дом, Санкт-Петербург)

The "Jubilee":

L. N. Tolstoy (Л. Н. Толстой) *Полное собрание сочинений в 90 томах, академическое юбилейное издание.* Под общей ред. В. Г. Черткова. Москва: Государственное издательство художественной литературы, 1928–58 [abbreviated in parenthetical citations *PSS*)] [1]

OLCE:

Leo Tolstoy, *On Life: A Critical Edition*, edited by Inessa Medzhibovskaya, translated by Michael Denner and Inessa Medzhibovskaya. Evanston, IL: Northwestern UP, 2019

OLAH:

Tolstoy's On Life (from the Archival History of Russian Philosophy) cross-referenced in this volume.

---

1   Unless qualified in each case when an alternative source is used, all references to Tolstoy's texts in Russian in this volume are to The Jubilee. Henceforth, all parenthetic references to Tolstoy's texts from the Jubilee edition in this volume cite PSS followed by the respective volume and page separated by a colon.

OLMT:

"On Life" in *On Life and Essays on Religion*. Leo Tolstoy. Tr. with and Intro. Aylmer Maude. London: Oxford UP, 1934: 2 - 167

PSS:

The Jubilee in parenthetical citations

Questions:

Questions of Philosophy and Psychology (Вопросы философии и психологии); the journal published by the Moscow Psychological Society

TVS:

Л. Н. Толстой в воспоминаниях современников, в 2-х томах. под редакцией Г. В. Красновой, К. Н. Ломунова, С. А. Макашиной, Н. Н. Фортунатова и др. Москва: Государственное издательство художественной литературы, 1978 /abbreviated *TVS I* and *TVS II* where Romans indicate volume 1 or volume 2 of this edition/

A Note on the Text and the Cover

All dates for events, publications, letters, personal and official correspondence within and from Russia before 1918, unless otherwise noted, refer to the Julian calendar then in effect in the territory of the Russian Empire.

All dates in the same period covering the writings, publications, and letters of Tolstoy's correspondents, critics, and translators in the West adhere to the Gregorian calendar, which is about twelve days later than the dates of the Julian calendar. An ellipsis without brackets indicates an omission or gap in the original. An ellipsis in square brackets indicates the editor's deletion.

We have stayed close to the modified Library of Congress Romanization system.

The image on the book's cover of Tolstoy mowing a meadow reproduces Ilya Repin's famous sketch of Tolstoy during the artist's first stay at Yasnaya Polyana. Tolstoy is drawn in 1880, just the same as he was while working for a widowed peasant, Anisya Kopylova, late in the summer of 1887, when *On Life* had just been sent to the printers. The injury a year earlier that is so closely associated with the story of the writing of *On Life* had occurred during one of these regular missions delivering hay to the same peasant.

Tolstoy's *On Life* in Critical Perspective

(And on This Book in Brief)

Inessa Medzhibovskaya
The New School

We think that it is *On Life*—more than any other work by Tolstoy—that deserves to be honored in an inaugural book forum addressed to *one individual work* of his philosophy—and not on a single work of his fiction, autobiography, or other genre. This volume is not focused on a single philosophical *problem* of Tolstoy's art and thought, as was, for example, one of the major collections of Russian idealism, released in 1912 by the publishing house Put' (Путь) under the title *On the Religion of Lev Tolstoy* (*О Религии Льва Толстого*). The 1912 volume investigated Tolstoy's religious persona, specifically the relation of his convictions concerning the Russian state, Russian Orthodoxy, and their institutions. Finding in Tolstoy a scriptural anarchist, a separatist of conscience, the authors of the 1912 collection explained, each in their own way, Tolstoy's strange and tragic status in Russia, while he was alive and posthumously: famous worldwide, excommunicated from the Church at home, a restless spiritual refugee in search of an eternal home.

Authors in this volume have carefully considered the conclusions of *On the Religion of Lev Tolstoy* alongside other critical studies of *On Life*. A brief summary of the existing scholarship is in order (and I skip here any commentary on the work of Tolstoy's translators or the editions of *On Life* prior to 1978, including the publication of the work by

A. I. Nikiforov in volume 26 of *The Jubilee* edition of Tolstoy: the topic is covered in *OLCE* and *OLAH,* see Abbreviations).

A breakthrough moment in the study of *On Life* is the Soviet-era historiography of Tolstoy's nonfictional works by Lydia Dmitrievna Opulskaya. In her full-size chapter on Tolstoy in 1887, *On Life* is described as the main work of the year and classified as a "philosophical tract": "Л. Н. Толстой в 1887 г. Философский трактат *О жизни*" (83–116). After the publication of this essay in 1979, the most significant Russian-language interpretations of *On Life* may be found in Natalia Kudriavaia's works on Tolstoy's pedagogy (Н. В. Кудрявая). She undertakes the task of recuperating Tolstoy's teaching on life following over a century of calumny mixed with neglect: "Up until now, Tolstoy's worldview has been characterized in the philosophical dictionary as non-scientific, contradictory, and therefore unclear" (Кудрявая 1993, 5).

Among Anglophone works, a relative step forward in the process of the scholarly appreciation of *On Life* may be found in the commentary made on the work in Andrzej Walicki's chapter "Tolstoy's Philosophy of Life," where he writes, for example, that in *On Life* "Tolstoy demanded the renunciation of 'individual welfare' and not personality as such" (Walicki 1979, 333). In the following decade, even when discussing Tolstoy's theology, approaches of literary scholars toward *On Life* are still cautious. Richard Gustafson criticizes Tolstoy for not implementing his basic philosophical concepts consistently and rather changing them frequently by inventing new concepts for each new work: "The unsystematic use of the names for 'basic concepts' is what makes his attempts at coherent presentations of his views difficult to grasp. Even his best philosophical work, *On Life*, suffers from these failings inherent in the method" (Gustafson 1986: 91). In his renowned study, Gustafson assumes a nonchronological and non-time-specific evaluation of Tolstoy's thought. Thus, arguments from *On Life* are adduced when interpreting *Anna Karenina* (Gustafson, 130–1) written ten years before *On Life* and when considering other earlier and later texts. Gustafson argues from the major tenets of Eastern Christian conceptions of sin and recovery from it through the union of reason and love. (For other brief mentions of *On Life* in his book, see also Gustafson 98, 148, 273).

It is true that, from work to work, Tolstoy keeps refining his philosophical vocabulary. As we have recently discovered while investigating the patterns and frequency of Tolstoy's use of various terms in *On Life*, he does so with exceeding exactitude, almost to a fault. We therefore should like to voice a contradiction regarding the question of Tolstoy's terminological inconsistency: Only Tolstoy could use his terms so obstinately and repeatedly, without appearing monotonous. (On the impressive consistency in Tolstoy's use of terminology in *On Life*, see *OLCE*, 22–4).

Although it does not look specifically at *On Life*, of the works of Western scholarship dedicated to the study of one work of Tolstoy's religious writing we should mention David Matual's study of Tolstoy's harmonization and commentary of the gospels (Matual 1992). This meticulous and disciplined work of textual scholarship and historical theology added important correctives regarding our understanding of Tolstoy's deliberate "errors" in reading the gospels and the creative misprisions of his theological and ontological hermeneutics.

A few years after the publication of Gustafson's book, of special note is Gary R. Jahn's focus on the divided self, space and time, the reversal of death and birth, and on themes of alienation and love in his comparison of "The Death of Ivan Ilyich" with *On Life* (Jahn 1993: 93–102).

Donna Orwin's comments on *On Life* explain that this work summarizes the results of his struggle between nature and reason in the following way: "Man would be moral not because he was natural, but because he was rational and free" (Orwin 1993, 162). The reader should also refer to pages 193–4, 242, and 248 of this study where the idea of rational consciousness is discussed.

In his now classic essay "Tolstoy Among the Philosophers" (2006), James Scanlan provided the first analysis of the coverage received by *On Life* in the pages of the periodicals of the Moscow Psychological Society.

The insufficiency of rationality, which Tolstoy realized all too strongly, leads Jeff Love to see in *On Life*, Tolstoy's "most purely philosophical work," a step toward Tolstoy's "anti-philosophical opposition to reflection" in his later tracts (Love, 141–6; 162–3).

Concerning *On Life* as the culmination of Tolstoy's conversion and a milestone in his philosophical evolution, including the genealogy of his signature terminology, see Chapter 12, "*On Life* and Conclusion," of my *Tolstoy and the Religious Culture of His Time* (2008): 333–57.

Daniel Moulin makes a shrewd analysis of Tolstoy's inclusion of his biting critique of Scribes and Pharisees in *On Life* in the interest of venturing a broader pedagogical perspective on the humanistic values in true education in his volume on Tolstoy written for Bloomsbury's pedagogical series (Moulin 2011, 67–70).

Rosamund Bartlett writes a succinct, excellent assessment of *On Life* within Tolstoy's biography of a "sectarian, anarchist, holy fool" (Bartlett 2011, 323). More recently, Irina Paperno offers an innovative reading of *On Life* in connection with Tolstoy's personal genres of self-narration (Paperno 2014, 131–34).

My introduction and notes in the new Critical Edition of *On Life* from Northwestern University Press (*OLCE*), furnish a detailed intellectual chronology of the work, situating it within Tolstoy's philosophical biography and its Russian intellectual milieu, while also extending the purview to the connections between *On Life* and the most significant figures and trends of the philosophical tradition as well as looking at the reception patterns of *On Life* (Medzhibovskaya 2019, 3–41; 187–211). The introductory essay to *Tolstoy's On Life (from the Archival History of Russian Philosophy) (OLAH)* provides an extensive coverage of responses to *On Life* discovered in the historical and institutional archives and in collections of private papers. Complementing *OLCE* and *OLAH*, the present volume is an attempt to broach further investigations of *On Life* in several important directions.

***

Following this introduction are five interpretive essays that were commissioned from leading historians of thought, philosophers, literary scholars, and Tolstoy specialists. These five essays undertake the study of Tolstoy in the assessment of Russian idealism of the late nineteenth century and early twentieth century both before and after 1917 by the émigré philosophers to be exiled from Soviet Russia on the "philosophical steamer" in 1922; the investigation of the debts of *On Life* to Kant and some of the traditions of eudemonia; and the exploration of Tolstoy's treatment of the problem of suffering and his position concerning doctrines of theodicy in *On Life*. Further chapters offer readings of *On Life* through the seemingly disparate but in fact inseparable viewpoints of science, spiritualism, and theater. The interpretive essays conclude with a coda regarding *On Life* and its handling of impersonal life from the perspective of the horror of philosophy.

In "Tolstoy and Russian Idealism," Randall Poole takes on an oft-quoted—and commonly uncritically received—passage found in one of Tolstoy's notebooks from 1879 that dates back to Tolstoy's "crisis" years during his conversion, where he writes about the gradations and types of idealism. There, Christ is named as the most perfect and accomplished of idealists, teaching men how to return to their spiritual home, flying upward to heaven. Tolstoy places himself at the bottom of the hierarchy, far below those who can fly like Christ, lower than monks, and even below the good idealists who do rise but only above the general niveau of the crowd. Poole extends these points of Tolstoy's self-criticism in several momentous directions—concerning "lived idealism," freedom of conscience, and the construction of the Kingdom of God—Tolstoy's treatment of which was perceived overall negatively and was subjected to what Poole calls the then-prevailing attitude of "withering critique" from various groups within Russia's developing tradition of idealism. Nikolai Grot, a longtime Chairman of the Moscow Psychological Society, was among the forerunners of this trend of critique of Tolstoy by the new idealism of the post-Kantian era in Russia. Poole focuses mainly on the later generation of Russian idealists, those who matured and came of age after the death of Grot and Soloviev at the turn of the century, the last generation of prerevolutionary Russian philosophers, whose work was published in key forums and periodicals of Russian idealism. In addition to the veterans, such as the journal *Вопросы Философии и Психологии* (*Questions of Philosophy and Psychology*; 1889-1917), the later forums included especially the following collections of essays: *Проблемы Идеализма* (*Problems of Idealism*; 1902), *Вехи* (*Signposts*; 1909), and the already mentioned *О Религии Льва Толстого* (*On the Religion of Lev Tolstoy*; 1912). Most important in this regard for Poole are the critical evaluations of Tolstoy's individualistic pursuit of the infinite borne out of his extreme impersonalism by such thinkers as Piotr Struve, Sergei Bulgakov, Nikolai Berdiaev, and Semyon Frank. Yet he also pays attention to the important interim correctives from the various points of "concrete spiritualism" offered by Piotr Astafiev, Aleksei Kozlov, Lev Lopatin, Nikolai Lossky, and Vasilii Zenkovsky; the claims of liberal statism put forward by Boris Chicherin and Struve; the expressions of Frank's later religious ontologism; and the idiosyncratic convictions of Soloviev's religious philosophy.

While many of the Russian thinkers who criticized Tolstoy's personalism were Leibnizians, his rationalistic optimism and his very choice of *разумное сознание* (reasonable consciousness) as the pivotal term of *On Life* in its relation to human happiness as interpreted by major traditions within critical philosophy, have remained insufficiently explained. In "The End of *On Life*: Kant with Tolstoy," Jeff Love turns to Kant's presence in *On Life*—which is both hidden and open. By doggedly adhering to the rhetoric of optimistic well-being, negotiating "between [a] holistic overview" and the perspectives of the "atomistic particular," Love argues, Tolstoy places his work within the discourse of eudemonia, albeit largely on the grounds of the German idealist tradition. (After Leibniz and Kant, this tradition includes, for Love, Weber and Heidegger.) Love translates *разумное сознание* as "rational consciousness," and in so doing goes against the grain of the traditional rendering of the term as "reasonable consciousness." His is a highly principled choice. Love sees in Tolstoy's deployments of terminology a kind of holistic syncretism rather than the doctrinaire agnosticism and bare bones spiritualism that *On Life* is so often mistaken to be promoting. According to Love, *On Life* mounts the narration of a somewhat nihilistic ontologism that strongly depends on the constantly shifting perspectives of the "I." There are many moods in this mind's "I," which displays a clear fascination with the elusive meanings and qualities of "things." Love sees no cause for despair over the closed-off metaphysical areas and the fault lines demarcating the limits of reason, the giving up on the things-in-themselves, along with the relinquishment of the unknowable "dead matter." Rather than signifying the dead ends of metaphysical cognition, there is a theme of freedom in Tolstoy's Kantian evocations, a yearning for surprise that lowbrow, mundane science cannot discern through its telescopes and microscopes. In this picture, reason is neither a shackle nor a limit; it is our liberator. Our subjugation to what reason commands makes us akin to a horse being guided by a rein: we can choose to resist and thrash around only to be geed up, and to continue on our course with either enjoyment or resignation. The choice is there, and Love sees the attraction of *On Life* in the open-ended stories that Tolstoy is inviting his readers to re-authorize.

In "Tolstoy's Implausible Theodicy: The Justification of Suffering in *On Life*," James Scanlan continues his earlier investigations of the critiques of *On Life* chiefly in *Questions of Philosophy and Psychology*. Scanlan asks: How can we judge the theodicy argument in the final chapters of *On Life*? Are these the products of Tolstoy's master storytelling or the tales of inadequacy coming from an amateur moralist posing as a philosopher?

Before proceeding to Leibniz and his reception in Russia, Scanlan tackles the "hoary problem of evil"; this route takes him back to one of the progenitors of eudemonia theory in all of its complexity, Epicurus. Lest it be forgotten, one of the starting points for Tolstoy's promotion of reasonable consciousness is the inability of animal consciousness to square the credit and debit of pleasure versus suffering.

Scanlan disagrees with Love (implicitly): though he also uses the translation "rational consciousness" rather than "reasonable consciousness," Scanlan understands Tolstoy's term differently because he needs a distinction from what Tolstoy condemns in *On Life* as *рассудочные объяснения* ("rational explanations"). Such explanations explain nothing about pain, suffering, and evil, Scanlan argues, in contrast to the explanations provided by rational consciousness, which is the consciousness of lived experience.

Rational consciousness knows for sure why there is suffering in life and how to deal with suffering, even if—rationally—suffering can be neither understood nor justified, no matter how convincingly philosophers may theorize the problem. Suffering is rational rather than irrational in that we get to live through it and come to terms with it, choosing either to understand it—to whatever degree is affordable to us—or to fail to do so.

Scanlan's Tolstoy promotes the quest for understanding, making us responsible for our suffering, and recommends enduring it with love and without bitterness. Scanlan does not buy this recipe. He cannot accept Tolstoy's presumption of guilt, of there being no innocent victims. On Tolstoy's scales of justice, sin—personal sin, the sin of all humanity—outweighs the possible sins of creation or the creator (the investigation of which is dropped in *On Life*, but is present in earlier texts such as *A Confession* and *What I Believe*). Scanlan insists that in individual human perception and in the perception of an individual philosopher, suffering and evil should always be judged in terms of cause and effect, or we lose track of real suffering, keeping it abstract. For a man of Tolstoy's passion, the promoter of nonviolence, the unredeemed tears of suffering covered up by clever terminology remain blemishes on his philosophy, and thus, given his Kantian swerve toward moral obligation and the search for loving bonds among humanity and between humanity and God, also blemishes on his intellectual conscience.

Tolstoy uses the term "spiritualism" almost interchangeably with "idealism" in *On Life*. A much lighter picture of the work, inspired by Tolstoy's many spiritualistic anecdotes scattered throughout its pages and in his fiction, is provided by Michael Gordin in "Tolstoy Sees Foolishness, and Writes . . . ." Gordin examines Tolstoy's involvement with spiritualism in its many guises (as science, as pseudo-science, as part of the developing tradition of psychological research in Russia, and as a significant artistic outlet).

Gordin outlines a detailed and objective picture of the involvement of key Russian scientists (Aleksandr Butlerov, Kliment Timiriazev, Ivan Sechenov) and social thinkers (Nikolai Danilevskii) in national discussions of the place of psychological and psychic study in contemporary science, specifically in relation to Darwinism. And he pays careful attention to the details of Tolstoy's knowledge of the spiritualist debate and its chief actors through a fascinating story of Tolstoy's interactions with Nikolai Vagner, "an interesting man," as Gordin calls him.

Interesting indeed: trained as an entomologist, Vagner was for decades one of the most active promoters of spiritualistic research in Russia, but was also a writer of very popular stories for children that he penned under the pseudonym "Кот-Мурлыка" (Cat-Purr). Vagner sought Tolstoy's attentions and never exited Tolstoy's orbit completely thanks to Nikolai Strakhov, a famous critic, who kept publishing works denouncing spiritualism—and Vagner too—tirelessly and steadily. Strakhov did that especially actively in the years when *On Life* was being written, banned, and then subjected to the aforementioned "withering critique," but, interestingly again, rarely from spiritualists. Gordin considers carefully any inviting bait that Tolstoy may have dangled before Vagner and other spiritualists (also mediums, hypnotizers, and theosophists) in his fiction and his journalism, where he covered science and its "real" life tasks. *On Life* was certainly one of these texts, but Tolstoy did not stop there.

Gordin examines the comedic extensions of *On Life* by undertaking a comparison of this work with Tolstoy's play *Плоды Просвещения* (*Fruits of Enlightenment*; 1889–90). Started as a dramatic piece to be staged and produced by Tolstoy's children as a form of domestic theater for the entertainment of family and friends that lampooned Vagner among other personages obsessed with spiritualistic phenomena, the play allows us to see Tolstoy's hilarious and rebellious artistic wit, which is also developed in *On Life*, in its send-up chapters that expose the trickery of the Scribes and other false prophets of knowledge.

In "Notes on Impersonal Life," Eugene Thacker explores the ramifications of Tolstoy's advocacy for impersonal life from the premonitious stances of the "horror of philosophy." In Tolstoy, Thacker notices the glimmers of catastrophism—feigned and real—that punctuate the posturing of much of postmodern thought, its unburied speculative corpses still shrugging off the dust of the remains of what used to be called life and what still remains misunderstood. But Thacker leaves us with the question of whether the "strange eternity" in Tolstoy's text is comparable to a dismal and acutely resigned pessimism of our age.

Do we need a "strange eternity," or any eternity? We hope this forum offers useful perspectives on Tolstoy's philosophical problems and the contradictory routes of his quest for truth that he probes in *On Life*—and can help us decide whether these apply to our own conditions and dilemmas.

Works Cited:

Bartlett, Rosamund. *Tolstoy: A Russian Life*. Boston: Houghton Mifflin, 2011

Gustafson, Richard F. *Leo Tolstoy. Resident and Stranger: A Study in Fiction and Theology*. Princeton, N. J.: Princeton UP, 1986

Jahn, Gary R. *The Death of Ivan Ilich. An Interpretation*. New York: Twayne Publishers, 1993

Кудрявая Н. В. «Лев Толстой как педагог: от народного учителя к учителю жизни». Л.Н. Толстой, *Педагогические сочинения*. Сост. Н. В. Кудрявая. Москва: ГЭОТАР-Медиа, 2010: 7-52

—. *Лев Толстой о смысле жизни. Образ духовного и нравственного человека в педагогике Л. Н. Толстого*. Москва: РИО ПФ «Красный пролетарий», 1993

Love, Jeff. *Tolstoy. A Guide for the Perplexed*. London: Continuum, 2008

Matual, David. *Tolstoy's Translation of the Gospels: A Critical Study*. Lewiston: The Edwin Mellen Press, 1992

Medzhibovskaya, Inessa. "Editor's Notes." *Tolstoy's On Life. A Critical Edition*. Ed. Inessa Medzhibovskaya. Tr. Michael Denner and Inessa Medzhibovskaya. Evanston, Ill.: Northwestern UP, 2019: 187-211 [abbreviated *OLCE*, 187-211]

—. "*On Life* in and beyond the Archive" in Inessa Medzhibovskaya, *Tolstoy's On Life (from the Archival History of Russian Philosophy)*. Toronto and DeLand, Fla.: the Tolstoy Society of North America, 2019

—. *Tolstoy and the Religious Culture of His Time: A Biography of a Long Conversion, 1845–1887*. Lanham, MD: Lexington Books, 2008

—. "Tolstoy's *On Life* and Its Times." *Tolstoy's On Life. A Critical Edition*. Ed. Inessa Medzhibovskaya. Tr. Michael Denner and Inessa Medzhibovskaya. Evanston, Ill.: Northwestern UP, 2019: 3-41[abbreviated OLCE, 3-41]

Moulin, Daniel. *Leo Tolstoy*. New York: Bloomsbury, 2011

Никифоров, А. И. "Комментарии <О жизни>." том 26. Произведения 1885 - 1889. редакторы, П. В. Булычев, Л. П. Гроссман, Н. К. Гудзий, А. И. Никифоров, Б. М. Эйхенбаум. Л. Н. Толстой. *Полное собрание сочинений в 90 томах, академическое юбилейное издание*. Под общей редакцией В. Г. Черткова. Москва: Государственное издательство «Художественная Литература», 1936: (*PSS* 26 : 748 - 844)

Опульская, Л. Д. *Лев Николаевич Толстой. Материалы к биографии с 1886 по 1892 год*. Москва: Наука, 1979

О религии Льва Толстого. Под ред. С. Н. Булгакова. Москва: Путь, 1912

Orwin, Donna Tussing. *Tolstoy's Art and Thought, 1847–1880*. Princeton, N.J.: Princeton UP, 1993.

Paperno, Irina. *"Who, What Am I?"Tolstoy Struggles to Narrate the Self*. Ithaca, N.Y.: Cornell UP, 2014

Scanlan, James "Tolstoy among the Philosophers: His Book *On Life* and Its Critical Reception." *Tolstoy Studies Journal* 18 (2006): 52–69

Tolstoy, L. N. (Толстой, Л. Н.) *Полное собрание сочинений в 90 томах, академическое юбилейное издание.* Под общей редакцией В. Г. Черткова. Москва: Государственное издательство художественной литературы, 1928–58 [abbreviated (*PSS*)]

Walicki, Andrzej. "Tolstoy's Philosophy of Life." *A History of Russian Thought from the Enlightenment to Marxism.* Tr. Hilda Andrews Rusiecka. Stanford, CA: Stanford UP, 1979: 332-35

Tolstoy and Russian Idealism

Randall A. Poole
The College of St. Scholastica

There are worldly people, heavy and wingless. . . . There are those whose wings grow equably and who slowly rise and fly: monks. There are light people, winged, who rise easily from among the crowd and again descend: good idealists. There are strong-winged ones who, drawn by carnal desires, descend among the crowd and break their wings. Such am I. . . . There are those who have heavenly wings, and purposely—from love of men—descend to earth (folding their wings) and teach men to fly. When they are no more needed they fly away: Christ.
— Толстой Л. Н., "Записная книжка №7" (28 октября 1879)[1]

The Moscow Psychological Society and Russian Idealism

In the three decades before the Russian Revolution, the most important center of the growth of Russian philosophy was the Moscow Psychological Society. Through his friendship with its chairman Nikolai Ia. Grot (1852–1899), Tolstoy became associated with the society, participated in its meetings, and contributed to its journal. *On Life*, generally regarded as the best exposition of his metaphysics,[2] was in part a product of his association with Grot and the society.[3] Psychological Society philosophers roundly criticized Tolstoy's version of metaphysical spiritualism for its impersonalism, for its rejection of the value of the distinctly human (as opposed to the divine), and for the anarchistic social philosophy that the great writer and moralist drew from it. At the same time, his "lived idealism" and his idealist conception of faith were powerful positive examples for them, Russia's "good idealists."

Established in 1885 at Moscow University, the Psychological Society owes its name to its founder, M. M. Troitsky (1835–1899), an empirical psychologist.[4] Within three years the society's direction was taken over by a group of idealist philosophers led by Grot, who was elected chair in January 1888, following his appointment as professor of philosophy at Moscow University in June 1886.[5] Among Grot's main colleagues were Vladimir S. Solvoviev (1853–1900), Sergei N. Trubetskoy (1862–1905), and Lev M. Lopatin (1855–1920). In his classic memoirs the Russian historian A. A. Kizevetter describes how in Moscow University circles at the time "all the talented young people occupied with philosophy stood in opposition to Troitsky and immersed themselves at once in metaphysical problems. At the head of these young people were Lopatin, Sergei Trubetskoy and—the most brilliant diamond of this philosophical generation—Vladimir Soloviev." They embraced Grot, "in all respects well-suited to this tight and friendly philosophical company. It was this company that captured the Psychological Society, transforming it into a philosophical society in the broad sense of the word" (Кизеветтер, 85).

With Grot's enthusiasm, pedagogical gifts, and organizational talents, the Psychological Society flourished. According to Lopatin, "it became one of our most popular centers of learning, not just in Moscow but in Russia more generally" (Лопатин 1911, 245–246). Grot, much loved by his colleagues, chaired the society until his death in May 1899. Lopatin succeeded him and directed the society until 1919. By the 1890s the Psychological Society had about 200 members, a number which remained fairly constant throughout its existence. In 1889 it began publication of Russia's first regular, specialized journal in philosophy, *Questions of Philosophy and Psychology* (*Вопросы Философии и Психологии*). Published five times a year until 1918, the journal was invaluable in promoting the development of a professional philosophical culture in Russia. In 1910, when the Psychological Society celebrated its twenty-fifth anniversary, one of its officers could evaluate it as a "profoundly significant fact in the life of Russian society, where in general philosophical questions could only relatively very recently become the object of free and, to the extent possible, objective discussion" (Виноградов, 261–2). By the end of its activity in 1922, when Russia's leading philosophers were deported, the Psychological Society had played an indispensable role in the growth of Russian philosophy.

From its early years the Psychological Society's first and main goal was to promote the autonomous development of Russian philosophy. To do this it needed to mount an effective theoretical challenge to positivism (the reigning worldview since the mid-nineteenth century), which asserted that the measure of reality was empirical experience: positively-given, external sense data. Against this reductionism, Psychological Society philosophers sought to defend the autonomy of philosophy by arguing that the positivist criterion of reality was far from exhaustive, and that what it did not exhaust comprised the special domain of philosophy. This domain was human consciousness itself, to the extent that it could be shown to be irreducible to sense experience (the positivist sphere). The critique of positivism and defense of the autonomy of philosophy thus took shape as a type of philosophy of consciousness. This was clearly an idealist enterprise, and the whole project has come to be known as Russian neo-idealism, "neo" because it was a revival and revision of classical German idealism, especially of Kantianism.

Tolstoy, Grot, and the Psychological Society

Tolstoy was involved in the work of the Moscow Psychological Society from its early years. At a meeting in March 1887 he delivered a synopsis of the long philosophical essay that he finished later that year (with Grot's editorial assistance), *On Life*.[6] He published three articles, including his major essay *What is Art?*, in *Questions of Philosophy and Psychology*.[7] In January 1894 the society elected him an honorary member.[8] He was an important influence, both positive and negative, in its development of Russian idealism. One simple measure of this is his presence in its seminal collection, *Problems of Idealism* (1902). Sergei Bulgakov, in his contribution to the volume, commends "the healthy ascetic kernel" in Tolstoy's teaching for its focus on moral and spiritual needs over material and sensuous ones (Bulgakov 2003, 102). In his essay Nikolai Berdiaev writes: "We have not adequately valued or even adequately understood the deep significance of Lev Tolstoy's critique of the existing order, made from the point of view of Christian idealism. After Tolstoy it is already impossible to relate to many things as indifferently as before; the voice of conscience more urgently demands that life be understood morally" (Berdiaev, 189–90). Semyon Frank turns to "that exquisite psychologist, Lev Tolstoy," to argue that since love of humanity is hardly a natural instinct it must be based on the moral law. "From this, the great thinker and moralist draws the conclusion that love of people requires, for its presence and strength, support in another feeling—in a religious-metaphysical sanction, in the love, inherent to people, for the Being personifying the moral law" (Frank 2003, 223).[9] These three philosophers would turn again and again to Tolstoy in their later writings.[10] Piotr Struve, the other famous Russian convert "from Marxism to idealism,"[11] did not refer to Tolstoy in his chapter of *Problems of Idealism*, but he regarded him, after Vladimir Soloviev's death in 1900, as Russia's greatest living religious thinker. He admired Tolstoy for his rejection of dogma and for his championing of the free, creative, and individual development of religious consciousness.[12]

Tolstoy's art and life showed what it was to be an idealist, far more compellingly for most people than abstract philosophical argument. Grot, in his lead editorial in the inaugural issue of *Questions of Philosophy and Psychology*, singled out Tolstoy, "with his new teaching of life and of the moral tasks of man," for his exceptional role in raising public interest in philosophy. "It may be," he suggests, "that no specialist has so strongly promoted the awakening of the philosophical spirit in Russian society as much as Count L. N. Tolstoy has indirectly done" (Грот 1889, xiii–xiv). Tolstoy was an idealist in the basic sense that moral ideals drove his feats of self-determination and shaped his self-conception. He was highly self-conscious of being an idealist in this sense and provided powerful accounts of it, most notably in *A Confession*. His fervent moral consciousness was itself testimony to the force of ideal aspirations over external reality and thus was its own type of refutation of positivism. It helped to spur the more theoretical articulation of Russian idealism in the Psychological Society. For society philosophers, human moral experience, so poignantly expressed by Tolstoy, entailed ontological or metaphysical conclusions about the nature of personhood and being, the explication and justification of which defined their neo-idealist program. As Grot put it in his editorial, the profound questions of life posed by Tolstoy "can be seriously and fundamentally clarified and resolved only on the ground of a new, comprehensive critique of general philosophical questions" (Грот 1889, xiv).

Tolstoy became associated with the Psychological Society through his friendship with Grot, whom he met in 1885.[13] In the first period of his philosophical development, Grot, like many of his contemporaries, was completely under the sway of positivism. By 1885, however, he was moving toward idealism, and Tolstoy's moral and religious ideas were a factor in the shift.[14] In a letter of 18 September 1910, within several weeks of his death, Tolstoy recalls that from their first meeting he and Grot liked each other. Grot, according to Tolstoy, was trying with difficulty to free himself from the "superstition of science" and from the "narrowness and, simply, stupidity of the materialist understanding of life." He turned to ethics, and through the "complex and long route of philosophy . . . came to the simple position recognized by every Russian peasant, even if illiterate, that *it is necessary to live for the soul.*"[15]

Tolstoy was right at least about the role of ethics in bringing about Grot's conversion to idealism. In the midst of his spiritual searching, Grot raised to the level of self-consciousness and the moral ideals that positivism masked under the guise of natural science. He came to recognize these ideals as central to human identity. Sokolov, the author of a valuable essay on Grot's philosophical development, expresses very well this new found awareness:

> With them [such ideals] are connected the most
> important moral interests of our existence, our ideas of
> the meaning of human and universal life, our concepts

of good and evil, of the moral and immoral, our belief in the sanctity of duty, in the possibility of happiness and in the triumph of justice. What remains of these, the best convictions of humanity, if they are deprived of real basis, if the ideals of truth, the good, and beauty, of which people have always dreamed, are only subjective phantoms, if the ideas of God, the soul, freedom of will, and immortality are empty, superstitious words? (Соколов, lxxiv)

And in asking with Grot, "Has nature really given us ideal aspirations only to make us victims of eternal self-deception and illusion?" (Соколов, lxxiv), Sokolov touches on a central insight of Russian neo-idealism: the presence of such ideals and their hold over us refute reductive positivism and its impoverished view of nature.

Decades earlier, Tolstoy had struggled with these very questions. From an early age he recognized that human beings are ideal-positing and ideal-driven creatures, and he wondered about what this meant for our place in, and for our understanding of, the natural world.[16] He would not resolve these and similar questions to his satisfaction until *A Confession*, but as early as 1852 he confided the following sentiments to his diary:

Nothing has so convinced me of the existence of God and of our relation towards Him, as the thought that the capacities of all animals are given them in accord with the needs which they have to satisfy. Not more, and not less. For what has the capacity to conceive of cause, eternity, infinity, and omnipotence, been given to man? The assumption of the existence of God is an hypothesis supported by indications [признаками]. And faith, in accordance with man's development, complements the correctness of that hypothesis. (*PSS* 46:139; qtd. in Maude, 1:87–88)

In late 1860, following the death of his brother Nikolai and at a time when his views were in flux, Tolstoy wrote in a similar vein: "Expediency [целесообразность] is the sole, the unalterable, law of nature, say the naturalists. But in the best manifestations of man's soul—love and poetry—it is absent. . . . Nature far overstepped her aim, having given man a need of poetry and love, if expediency is really her sole law" (*PSS* 48:31; qtd. in Maude, 1:216; translation modified). Considerations such as these convinced Grot and other Russian philosophers that positivism was an untenable worldview and that idealism better accorded with the full range and depths of human experience. The intellectual path that Struve, Bulgakov, Berdiaev and Frank traversed "from Marxism to idealism" was only the most famous of such conversions.[17]

Grot's Critique

The positive role of Tolstoy's "lived," moral idealism in the development of Russian philosophical idealism is a topic to which we will return. But soon after his religious conversion, which culminated in 1878–1879 as he was writing *A Confession*, Tolstoy moved toward an impersonalistic metaphysical spiritualism, which he expounded in his philosophical tract *On Life*. Grot, despite his friendship and esteem for Tolstoy, was highly critical of his metaphysical spiritualism and its implications. His criticisms were far-reaching; they both drew on earlier idealist critiques of Tolstoy and helped to shape later ones.[18] In his widely read 1893 essay "The Moral Ideals of Our Time (Friedrich Nietzsche and Lev Tolstoy)," he argued that the main contribution of both the German and Russian thinkers was, ironically, their extreme positions: in taking their theoretical views to their logical conclusion, they exposed more clearly the strengths and weaknesses of their ideas (Грот 1893).[19] Grot focuses on the weaknesses. As the root of all Nietzsche's errors is in his extreme materialism, he writes, "so Tolstoy's main mistake is in his extreme and narrow idealism and spiritualism. . . . In our view, Count Tolstoy's main mistake, like Nietzsche's, is in rejecting the profound *dualism* of human nature that forms the basis of all Christian metaphysics" (Грот 1893, 149–50).

True, in *On Life* Tolstoy draws a distinction (the central one of the book) between our "animal" and "reasonable" consciousness, but as Grot indicates this opposition is only a phenomenal one for Tolstoy, meaning that for him our fundamental nature consists in the spiritual reality of reasonable consciousness (Грот 1893, 150). Though Grot does not develop it, his classification of the great writer as an "extreme spiritualist" was an important point that resonated among other Russian idealists.

Grot's classification successfully captures the essence of Tolstoy's metaphysics. His spiritualism (a type of pantheism) supposes that reasonable consciousness is the only substantial reality. In *On Life*, his position is that reasonable consciousness (разумное сознание) is nothing less than God or divine *logos* (разум), which he also calls, simply, "true life" (Tolstoy 1934, chaps. 9–10, 14). Reasonable consciousness is the impersonal, divine spirit of love in man. It is the true human self—which identification tends to efface the distinction between human and divine. Our task is to liberate our higher divine self by subjecting our lower animal self ("animal personality") to reason, which is also the law of love (Tolstoy 1934, chaps. 22–33). Years later Tolstoy succinctly formulated his doctrine in his essay *The Law of Love and the Law of Violence* (1908). There he claims that Christian teaching acknowledges love to be "metaphysically the origin of everything" and "the essence of human life." According to him: "The teaching amounts to saying that what we call 'our self,' or our life, is really the divine principle, limited in us by our body, and manifesting itself as love, and that therefore the true life of each man, divine and free, expresses itself as love" (Tolstoy 1987a, 172–73).

Grot's essay "The Moral Ideals of Our Time" was written largely for a popular audience. By the time of its publication other Russian philosophers had already subjected *On Life* to withering critique.[20] In his essay Grot was content to draw the following general implications from Tolstoy's spiritualism:

> Having recognized the reason and spirituality of humanity, Tolstoy very soon forgets the constant presence in us of another nature, an animal and material

one. That's why our writer is so inclined to believe in the absolute goodness [доброкачественность] of human nature and in the possibility of man becoming perfect and good [благой], independent of any external norms of action. The church's teaching about sin and redemption is foreign to Tolstoy. He does not pose the question whether it is possible to find in this teaching some deep *philosophical* meaning, apart from its religious-dogmatic one. (Грот 1893, 150)

Grot was not criticizing Tolstoy merely from the church's perspective; he himself was not dogmatic in his religious views, and was writing in part to appease powerful conservative influences in precarious times for a new and independent philosophical journal. Later Russian idealists would return to the question of Tolstoy's metaphysical spiritualism, exploring it in more depth and generally finding it to be highly problematic.

Grot also pursued another line of criticism, focusing not so much on the nature of Tolstoy's metaphysics as on its cultural and social implications. His underlying argument is that Tolstoy's spiritualistic anthropology (conception of human nature) cannot sustain a genuine, liberal theory of progress. In this Grot helped to set the agenda for the Psychological Society's theoretical development of Russian liberalism, an integral aspect of its work.[21] One place where he advances this general approach is his response to Tolstoy's 1884 tract *What I Believe*. Despite its popularity, he thought the work had its weak sides, namely: 1) an extreme radicalism that rejects the necessity of compromise in human society, in conditions of imperfect moral development; 2) a lack of objectivity in Tolstoy's tendency to select the facts that suit him, while ignoring those that contradict him; and 3) an absence of historical criteria, which reinforces Tolstoy's radicalism in censuring the external forms of Christianity. "Tolstoy," Grot writes, "in general conflates the ideal with its fulfillment and with the degree of possible practical approximation to it" (Шенрок, 42).[22] This criticism underlies the liberal critique of utopianism that would take fuller shape in the thought of Psychological Society philosophers such as Evgenii Trubetskoy and Pavel Novgorodtsev. Despite his reservations, Grot deeply respected Tolstoy for helping to recover the higher ideals that both of them believed contemporary society had lost. Grot defended him unconditionally against charges of heresy, adding that for the philosopher, heresy does not exist, "only different degrees of approximation to truth." Tolstoy himself was a thinker "who has acquired a high degree of approximation to truth and who has undermined at root the philosophical arguments of atheists and narrow materialists" (Шенрок, 43).

In "The Moral Ideals of Our Time," Grot expands his incipient liberal critique of Tolstoy. He sharply opposes Tolstoy's rejection of the external organization of society and forms of culture. Art, science, religion and the state (государственность) are, he assures his readers, permanent features of the human condition; only their forms will change. Not only do they (and other cultural and civic forms) concretely embody or represent such ideals as beauty, truth, the good, justice, and the sacred, but (to extend slightly Grot's argument) they are necessary instruments of the ever fuller realization of these ideals. They are, in short, necessary instruments of progress. To this end, Grot wished also to encourage the growth of Russian civil society: guardedly he calls for "the strengthening of external public activity in the form of state organization." Rounding out his criticism of Tolstoy's ethical and social thought, he writes: "The true task of the moralist is not to destroy all the historical forms of humanity's spiritual existence, but to strive to infuse new content into them, to put each in its own place, and where necessary to show the shortcomings of one and the advantages of another" (Грот 1893, 152–53). His reference to putting each form in its own place is a defense of the necessary autonomy and legitimate rights of the distinct spheres of human experience and activity, and a warning against their conflation or the hypostatization of one at the expense of another.[23] This, too, will become a main principle of liberalism among Psychological Society idealists.[24] Grot expresses it here in concluding that the genuine moral ideal consists in reconciling the external and internal, the material and spiritual, science and religion, knowledge and faith, "pagan" and "Christian" (Грот 1893, 153).

Throughout, his underlying concern is the fullest possible development and self-realization of the human person, the foundational liberal value. In his view, Tolstoy's teaching ultimately undermines this value: "Professing the most sympathetic moral ideals, he tries to uproot the human person from the whole ground on which it has grown, from the ground of its religious, scientific, philosophic and social traditions" (Грот 1893, 153).

"Lived Idealism," Conversion, and Faith in the Infinite

For all his criticism of Tolstoy, Grot believed that he played an important developmental role in Russian philosophical and religious thought. This role reflected not primarily *On Life*, but rather his "lived idealism" and his powerful presentation of it in *A Confession*.[25] Though Tolstoy's famous account of his religious conversion was banned from publication in Russia, it circulated widely in one form or another and was, according to Medzhibovskaya, "debated nationwide in private conversations and correspondence" (Medzhibovskaya 2008, 250). Its impact was, of course, tremendous. In 1885 Grot sent one of his essays (by way of self-introduction) to Tolstoy, dedicating it "to the deeply respected author of *A Confession*" (Medzhibovskaya 2008, 276). Vasilii Zenkovsky (1881–1962) and Pavel Florensky (1882–1937), two Russian theologians (and Orthodox priests) whose mature religious outlooks were very different than Tolstoy's, were deeply affected by *A Confession*. Florensky was so moved that in 1899 he wrote to Tolstoy asking him how he should live his life (Pyman, 23). Zenkovsky, presumably many years after he first read it, wrote: "There is hardly another document in world literature that is written as forcefully as Tolstoy's *Confession*, every word of which is full of flaming, elemental force" (Zenkovsky, 1:389).

Tolstoy's conversion was a gradual process that took place as he acquired, by the late 1870s, a deeper understanding of the meaning of his virtually lifelong idealism. It is well known that all his life Tolstoy was preoccupied with the task of self-perfection. He was keenly aware that self-perfection involved the positing of ideals, and that all his efforts at self-determination were made possible by them. As early as 1847, his last year at the University of Kazan, he had acquired, as he later wrote in *Adolescence,* "an ecstatic worship of the ideal of virtue, and the conviction that a man's destiny is continually to perfect himself."[26] In the first chapter of *A Confession,* Tolstoy says that by the age of sixteen he had lost his childhood faith in Orthodox Christianity. His "only real faith" at that time was a general belief in perfecting himself—intellectually, physically, morally (Tolstoy 1987a, 21). His self-conscious striving toward perfection was what made him an idealist, though he did not come to a fuller appreciation of the metaphysical implications of his moral idealism until his conversion, which resulted in a firm and steadfast faith; before then he experienced alternating periods of belief and doubt. After his conversion, he generalized his idealist pursuit of self-perfection into one of his fundamental religious principles: the Kingdom of God is within you, through infinite self-perfection according to the ideal that Jesus taught: "Be perfect even as your Father in heaven is perfect" (Matthew 5:48).[27]

Tolstoy's conversion was preceded by a spiritual crisis in the mid-1870s. The crisis was precipitated by Tolstoy's loss of faith in the meaning of life. In despair he wrote, "The truth was that life is meaningless," given the inevitable "reality of suffering and death: of complete annihilation" (Tolstoy 1987a, 30). Much of *A Confession* retraces Tolstoy's path to his recovery of faith in the meaning of life, his search for an answer to the question, "is there any meaning in my life that will not be annihilated by the inevitability of death?" (Tolstoy 1987a, 35). First he realizes that such meaning cannot be found using the finite methods of rational, scientific reason or knowledge. At one point he refers to Kant on the impossibility of proving the existence of God: "Kant had shown me this and I had fully understood that it cannot be proven" (Tolstoy 1987a, 63). Tolstoy's overall approach does suggest a broad similarity with Kant's argument that "antinomies" are the inevitable result of attempting to use the finite concepts and categories of theoretical reason (which apply only to the phenomenal world in space and time) to resolve infinite metaphysical questions.[28] After intense spiritual and intellectual struggle, Tolstoy recognizes that finite life can have no meaning apart from the infinite, and that only faith can "give an infinite meaning to the finite existence of man, a meaning that is not destroyed by suffering, deprivation or death" (Tolstoy 1987a, 54).

What are Tolstoy's grounds for faith in the infinite? It is clear that he discovers them in the infinite, absolute ideal that all along had been the motive or determinant of his efforts at perfectibility. "I returned," he writes, "to the idea that the single most important aim of my life is to improve myself," that is, to live according to the will of God.

> I returned to the conviction that I could find the manifestation of this will in something that had been hidden from me for a long time, in what humanity had worked out long ago for its own guidance. In other words I returned to a belief in God, in moral perfection, and to the tradition which had given life a meaning. Only the difference now was that whereas before I had accepted all this unconsciously, I now knew that I could not live without it. (Tolstoy 1987a, 65–66)

Thus, Tolstoy's conversion came about with his recognition that faith is born of the infinite ideal, one form of which is the moral law as experienced in self-determination and in the practice of perfectibility, or through what Kant called "practical reason." Tolstoy came to faith when he realized that it comes from within the human person, most poignantly in acts of self-determination—not externally through miracle, revelation, or dogma.

In his subsequent religious writings Tolstoy often returns to this understanding of faith. His focus is always on the infinite. In "Religion and Morality" (1893), he writes that "religion is the relationship man establishes between himself and the infinite, never-ending universe, or its origin and first cause" (Tolstoy 1987a, 142). In *What is Religion and of What Does Its Essence Consist?* (1902), he defines religion as our consciousness of and relationship to the infinite, which conscious relationship is established by reason. As a result, genuine faith is never irrational or contrary to reason (Tolstoy 1987a, 89, 98, 104). In *The Law of Love and the Law of Violence* (1908), one of his best essays, he describes faith as "the most essential and natural condition of human life" and defines it again as "the awareness of one's relationship to the Infinite" (Tolstoy 1987a, 204–05). In these and other writings, Tolstoy's premise is that faith comes from awareness or consciousness of the infinite, either through moral experience or through what might be called "cosmological experience," that is, experience of infinite being, as in the reference above to "the infinite, never-ending universe." His essays on religion and ethics do not dwell on the cosmological mystery, but his fiction conveys it as few other works in world literature. He sometimes used the idea of Nirvana to express it.[29] It bears emphasizing that for Tolstoy faith or religion is *not* the source of the infinite ideal; rather human experience of the infinite ideal is the source of faith. He believed that such experience, and therefore faith also, is natural to humanity. His religion was a type of natural theology.

Tolstoy's Religious Individualism

Russian idealists, even those who otherwise were sharply critical of Tolstoy (most were), generally had deep respect for the inner process of his conversion and for his idealist conception of faith. In the important 1912 collection *On the Religion of Lev Tolstoy* (*О Религии Льва Толстого*), Sergei Bulgakov and Vasilii Zenkovsky both underscore the individual nature of Tolstoy's religious consciousness, individual not in the sense that it was peculiar to Tolstoy alone but rather in the sense of its common meaning for all persons as individuals. True faith, Tolstoy showed, comes from within, through individual self-determination according to infinite, absolute ideals. Faithful religious consciousness is thus by its very nature an individual achievement. Four years earlier Semyon Frank, in two short but philosophically rich essays on Tolstoy, also pursued this interpretation of his religious significance.

Bulgakov (1871–1944) may well have been the most important Orthodox theologian of the twentieth century. In his opening chapter of *On the Religion of Lev Tolstoy*, the young religious philosopher declares:

In Tolstoy we have before us a historical fact of colossal importance, full of the deepest meaning: the greatest genius of the epoch, not only among his own people but in all of humanity, utterly devoting himself to the search for the religious meaning of life and sacrificing himself upon the altar of religion. . . . Tolstoy stands before the world as a living symbol of religious searching, as a testament to religion in our epoch of the unprecedented triumph of the mechanistic worldview. (Булгаков 1912, 2–3)

What Bulgakov values most about Tolstoy's religion is its appeal to personal conscience and to everyone's personal responsibility before God; it has helped to bring about nothing less than the spiritual birth of the human personality in an age of materialism and external necessity (Булгаков 1912, 5). Despite his fulsome acknowledgment of Tolstoy's role in promoting the contemporary religious awakening, he has very little regard for the actual content of Tolstoy's religious and ethical teachings, which he rejects as more nihilistic than religious (Булгаков 1912, 7). Ironically this helps Bulgakov to make his main point. Tolstoy, with his feat of religious self-determination, sacrificed his artistic genius and became "a mediocre theologian and moralizing public intellectual" (Булгаков 1912, 16, 23). The artist was capable of works such as *Anna Karenina*, the teacher and moralist was capable merely of works such as *The Kingdom of God Is within You*, which pale in comparison (Булгаков 1912, 22). Yet this very sacrifice reveals all the power of faith and of the inner ideal that is its source. This is why, Bulgakov writes, "the enormous spectacle of the self-immolation of an artistic genius carries transcendent religious meaning" (Булгаков 1912, 24).

Zenkovsky gives even more emphasis to Tolstoy's religious individualism, calling him a "mighty representative of contemporary individualism" (Зеньковский, 28). In his account, Tolstoy's individualism consists both in his self-determination and in the powerful example that it set:

> Through grueling work on the spirit, through arduous struggle with himself, the religious personality matured and developed in him, and Tolstoy's greatest contribution, his unforgettable significance for contemporary culture lies precisely in his bold, heartfelt struggle—which often revealed his genius—for the religious understanding of the world, for the religious approach to life. (Зеньковский, 28)

Getting carried away with his assessment, Zenkovsky—contradicting Bulgakov in the same volume and lacking his subtlety—goes on to say that religious creativity was Tolstoy's real genius and that it was more valuable and important than everything else he gave to culture (Зеньковский, 28). His next assertion may seem as exaggerated or just fanciful: "Tolstoy was a mystic" (Зеньковский, 29). With this term, Zenkovsky hopes to capture Tolstoy's spiritual sensitivity to experience of the infinite (both in the moral and cosmological modes). "Tolstoy came to religion," he writes, "led by the natural consciousness of the divine [естественное Богознание] that burns in every mystical nature" (Зеньковский, 30). This consciousness, he continues, explains why Tolstoy had no need of revelation or of the church. His "mysticism" was, in other words, an aspect of his individual religious consciousness. Zenkovsky points to its negative sides, such as Tolstoy's refusal to consider the possible truthfulness of another's religious experience, in short, his "intolerance" (Зеньковский, 30). While the future priest (and major historian of Russian philosophy) recognizes that "each of us can and must go freely to God" and that "each of us must individually apperceive all the fullness of religious reality," nonetheless his own point of view is that "individual religious experience must always be corroborated by the Church" (Зеньковский, 32). The rest of his essay is devoted to the problem of immortality in Tolstoy, which problem is part of the more general paradox that Tolstoy combined his individualism with metaphysical impersonalism (see below).

Decades later, Zenkovsky would call Frank (1877–1950) "the most outstanding among Russian philosophers generally" (Zenkovsky,

2:853). Four years before Bulgakov and Zenkovsky, Frank advanced the thesis of Tolstoy's individualism. In "L. N. Tolstoy's Ethical Teaching," he argues that Tolstoy's worldview combines dogmatic moralism and individualism, the first element being false and shallow, the second true and profound (Франк 1996c, 437–438). In a certain sense Tolstoy's anarchistic social ethics, for all its dogmatism, is an example of his individualism: in essence the anarchistic ideal is an individualistic one, and Tolstoy championed it "in the name of the freedom and self-determination of the person." But Frank dwells rather on Tolstoy's individualism in his understanding of religion "as the living, personal, inner relation of a human being to the divine." Like Zenkovsky after him, Frank associates Tolstoy's individualism with mysticism, but (perhaps wisely) does not develop the connection. More interesting is his dismissal of the "new religious consciousness" (promoted by Dmitrii Merezhkovsky and other participants in the St. Petersburg Religious-Philosophical Meetings, 1901–1903). In his estimation the only authentic new religious consciousness is Tolstoy's. It is first of all *individualistic*: "it searches for and finds God . . . only in the great mystery of the human soul's consciousness of the divine" (Франк 1996c, 438).

Frank brings his argument to culmination in another 1908 essay, "Lev Tolstoy and the Russian Intelligentsia." Here he draws a contrast between the intelligentsia's "social" worldview and the religious worldview. He glosses "social" as "the tribal or herd instinct" (an unfair and polemical point, this being a year before *Vekhi* [*Вехи*]). The religious worldview, by contrast, is based "on the instinct of individual being and, at the same time, on the feeling of a connection to the cosmos" (Франк 1996a, 442). Individualism, Frank continues, is "the premise and inner condition of the religious-metaphysical worldview" (Франк 1996a, 443). By individualism, he means self-perfection (as he stressed in "L. N. Tolstoy's Ethical Teaching") or, as he puts it here, "spiritual work" on oneself, "the constant work of self-knowledge and self-deepening" (Франк 1996a, 443, 444). And as an example of how the religious-metaphysical worldview emerges from individualism— understood in the idealist sense of individual self-determination and perfectibility according to absolute or infinite ideals—he commends to the reader *A Confession* (Франк 1996a, 443). In this period of his intellectual development, Frank described his own outlook as "religious individualism"; clearly his understanding of Tolstoy had a part in shaping it.[30] In his contribution to *Vekhi*, he meant essentially the same thing when he used the term "religious humanism" (Frank 1994, 155).

Faith and Freedom of Conscience

In tsarist Russia, with its despotic union of church and state, Tolstoy's idealist, individualistic approach to faith was a major breakthrough. Maude, who had a keen understanding of the spiritual affairs of both Russia and Tolstoy, remarked that *A Confession* was a rare brave deed because its author challenged "both the authorities that compelled the allegiance of his contemporaries": the rampant materialism of the intelligentsia on the one hand and "the theory and practice of the Orthodox Russian Church (and incidentally of all established Churches)" on the other (Maude, 1:410). The "greatness of his service," Maude continues, was in helping to persuade people that "no progress was possible without an emancipation from the petrified ecclesiasticism that masqueraded as religion" (Maude, 2:39). Tolstoy offered a different foundation for faith:

> By arriving at the conclusion that we are parts of a moral universe, and that only in so far as we discern that order and adjust ourselves to it has life any meaning and purpose that is not defeated by death, Tolstoy reached the ultimate root of religion. Through strife and suffering, to have found it by his own efforts, and to have proclaimed it in the teeth of those who denounced him as a heretic and atheist as well as those who sneered at him as a superstitious dotard, is an achievement entitling him to rank among the prophets. (Maude, 2:37–38)[31]

While it may not rank him among the prophets, it was an impressive achievement. Part of its importance, as Maude implies, consisted in Tolstoy's defense of freedom of conscience. According to Medzhi-bovskaya, with *A Confession* Tolstoy "drew the attention of the whole nation to the precedent he set for wrestling with the oppressive state and its ideology for freedom of conscience" (Medzhibovskaya 2008, 250). This struggle occupied him in many subsequent works and was dramatically epitomized by his excommunication in 1901. It is clear that freedom of conscience, in its core meaning of the individual's right to self-determination according to freely recognized ideals, was essential to—indeed a condition of—Tolstoy's idealist conception of faith.

The defense of freedom of conscience was a top priority of the Psychological Society. We have seen that Grot defended Tolstoy against charges of heresy. His editorials in *Questions of Philosophy and Psychology* stressed tolerance and free competition of diverse intellectual currents on the pages of the journal, all the more so in that it was Russia's only philosophical journal (Грот 1890, vi).[32] *Problems of Idealism* was conceived in 1901—the same year that Tolstoy was excommunicated by the Holy Synod—as a symposium in defense of liberty of conscience and its importance in liberalism. Lev Lopatin, in his capacity as chair of the Psychological Society, felt obliged to attach a short preface to the volume, which preface reads in part: "Following in its editions the principle of impartiality with regard to different philosophical currents, the Society in this way expresses its faith in the undoubted triumph of truth, which in and of itself carries the force of its own confirmation, and of its abiding significance and supremacy" (Lopatin 2003, 79).

Boris Chicherin and Vladimir Soloviev, the two greatest philosophers of nineteenth-century Russia and prominent members of the Psychological Society, were tireless champions of freedom of conscience.[33] As early as 1857 Chicherin called it "the first and most sacred right of a citizen" (Chicherin, 134–35).[34] In this "conservative liberal" period of his development, he still qualified this right in important ways, but by 1879, in his book *Science and Religion* (Наука и религия), he recognized it as an absolute principle and as the very basis of human dignity: "freedom of conscience is the inviolable sanctuary of the human soul, which the state has no right to infringe, and freedom of thought, even with all its errors, constitutes the necessary condition of development" (Чичерин 1901, 231). Similarly, by about 1880—in *Lectures on Godmanhood* and *Critique of Abstract Principles*[35]—it had become an essential principle in Soloviev's religious philosophy, the very condition of Godmanhood (Богочеловечество) or of humanity's divine potential and vocation, the ideal of our self-realization in and union with God. The publication of these major works by Chicherin and Soloviev roughly coincided with the appearance of *A Confession*, a concurrence that seems to have been a threshold in the public defense of freedom of conscience in late imperial Russia.[36]

Soloviev, widely recognized as Russia's greatest religious philosopher by the time of his death in 1900, was probably the most visible member of the Psychological Society. He and Tolstoy were very different thinkers; their intellectual and personal animosity is well known.[37] Yet both shared a liberal theological approach that emphasized human agency, autonomy, and responsibility in realizing the Kingdom of God, though they had almost diametrically opposed conceptions of this ultimate ideal, as we will see. Tolstoy rejected miracle, revelation, and dogma as impediments to self-determination and the free realization of faith from within (i.e., faith in the proper sense of the word). Soloviev may not have utterly rejected them, but he certainly downplayed their role, for the same reasons as Tolstoy.[38] Both thinkers understood, with Dostoevsky, that miracles can enslave. In *Lectures on Godmanhood*, Soloviev deplored what he called "the dark fanaticism that holds to a single particular revelation" (Solovyov, 36–37). He did not, like Tolstoy, reject the idea of the incarnation of God, but his Christology is distinctly philosophical and universalistic. He maintained that "strictly speaking, the incarnation of Divinity is not miraculous, that is, it is not alien to the general order of being" (Solovyov, 157). In his 1891 speech "The Collapse of the Medieval Worldview," he commented on Luke 9: 49–56 as follows: "James and John did not know the spirit of Christ, and they did not know it just because they believed above all in His external miraculous power. Such power there was, but it was not the essential thing" (Frank 1950, 62). The Russian philosopher closest to Soloviev, Evgenii Trubetskoy, expressed the spirit of his Christology in writing: "Christ's complete sacrifice saves man not as sorcery from outside, but as spiritual influence *liberating him from inside* and transforming his nature only on the condition of the *autonomous* self-determination of his will" (Трубецкой, 204).

Two Types of Idealism

Tolstoy's idealist conception of faith bears a strong resemblance to Kant's "moral religion," an affinity that has prompted recent Tolstoy scholarship to explore the Kantian character of Tolstoy's thought and the extent of Kant's actual influence on the Russian thinker.[39] Tolstoy read the *Critique of Practical Reason* in 1887 with "joyous rapture," regarding it as a "temple" of wisdom (Jahn, 62). As the second epigraph for the book he wrote that year, *On Life*, he chose Kant's lines (in the conclusion to the second critique) expressing "wonder and awe" for "the starry heavens above me and the moral law within me"—a famous formula of the moral and cosmological modes of experiencing the infinite. In the *Critique of Practical Reason* and other works,[40] Kant advanced his concept of moral theology. First, he defined morality as the capacity for self-determination (autonomy of the will) according to consciousness of "ought" (duty, the moral law, or the categorical imperative).[41] Second, he held morality to be the foundation of religious faith, both in the sense that it entails a theistic metaphysics (which he formulated in his postulates of immortality and the existence of God) and that faith emerges through moral experience. The similarity between Tolstoy's idealist conception of faith and Kant's is obvious, apart from the question of actual influence. By about the time of *On Life*, Tolstoy embraced Kant's philosophy (insofar as he understood it) as his own, in the literal sense that the German philosopher confirmed his own ideas and validated his own experiences. As Jahn writes, "the ideas of Kant which Tolstoj came to value so highly were nearly all thoughts which he had previously worked out for himself" (Jahn, 67).

Kantianism (not to be confused with neo-Kantianism) was one of two main idealist currents in the Psychological Society, especially among the liberal theorists.[42] Even Chicherin, generally regarded as Russia's foremost Hegelian philosopher, moved decisively toward Kant beginning in the 1870s.[43] The second current was spiritualism or panpsychism, a monistic metaphysics stipulating that all reality is spirit or mind. In *On Life*, as we have seen, Tolstoy adopted a version of metaphysical spiritualism, which he attempted to combine with the Kantianism of his idealist approach to faith. Thenceforth these two types of idealism will remain incongruous elements of his thought and will never be reconciled. They might be seen as a later example of Isaiah Berlin's "hedgehog" and "fox" thesis (Berlin). The hedgehog is now the impersonalistic, monistic spiritualist, while the fox is the individualistic, pluralistic Kantian.

Spiritualism traces its modern origins to Leibnizian monadology. Its main representatives in Russia were Aleksei Kozlov, Lev Lopatin, and Nikolai Lossky.[44] In his "system of concrete spiritualism," which was fairly typical of the movement as a whole, Lopatin surmised that free creative spirit is the substantial essence of all being. We discover it in our inner psychic world, in our immediate experience of the active, goal-oriented, creative self.[45] If the world is spiritual in its essence and accords with the demands of reason, then it must be understood as a teleological process oriented toward the free, creative realization of the good. This objective ideal of creation is also our own moral ideal, and the realization of the moral world-order depends on us (Лопатин 1890). "Indeed one and the same force," Lopatin writes in his philosophical credo, "drives the world and constitutes the deepest root of our individual spirituality" (Лопатин 1912a, 187). Tolstoy's position, in certain passages of *On Life*, seems very close to Lopatin's.[46] For example: "Our knowledge of the world results from the consciousness we have of our own aspiration towards good and of the necessity of subjecting our animal self to reason for the attainment of that good." And further: "The knowledge of anything whatever is for us the bringing to bear on it of our consciousness that life is a striving after good which is only attainable by submission to the law of reason" (Tolstoy 1934, chap. 13, 58-59).

The similarity is also noticeable on Lopatin's side. In December 1911, the Psychological Society celebrated the thirtieth anniversary of the beginning of Lopatin's career. On this occasion he provided a concise statement of his philosophical ideas. He distinguished between two opposing worldviews in the history of thought. According to one, "our inner mental world, our self, our consciousness and will are only phenomena, only a fleeting mirage." According to the other (his own), "only in the soul, only in the immediate experiences of our inner self, is actual reality given to us" (Лопатин 1912a, 186). In *On Life* Tolstoy wrote that "there are only two strictly logical views of life." According to one, "consciousness itself is nothing but a product of inanimate matter, a phantom, which appears and disappears leaving no trace or meaning." According to the other (his own), "life is only that which I am conscious of in myself" (Tolstoy 1934, chap. 27, 114). It is not clear whether the similarity in these passages (and others) is the result only of a shared general philosophical approach (spiritualism) or of Tolstoy's influence on Lopatin.

What is clear is that Tolstoy and the Psychological Society spiritualists were divided over the issue of personalism. The "concrete" element in Lopatin's "system of concrete spiritualism" designates his emphasis on persons, i.e., on human beings as morally responsible agents and as ontologically-grounded spiritual entities. In general, Russian spiritualism or panpsychism has been closely associated with philosophical personalism.[47] By contrast, as we have seen, Tolstoy's spiritualism was impersonalistic. It is striking that the first two (devastating) critiques of *On Life* to be published in *Questions of Philosophy and Psychology* were made by Russian spiritualists who objected, among other things, to Tolstoy's impersonalism: P. E. Astafiev and A. A. Kozlov. They found abhorrent his rejection of the value of the individual human person, and of the cultural values that promote its development, for the sake of divine "reasonable consciousness."[48] In arriving at his metaphysical impersonalism Tolstoy was decisively influenced by Schopenhauer, who saw individual being as an illusory and baneful consequence of spatiotemporal (phenomenal) existence.[49]

The combination of Kantianism and spiritualism in Tolstoy's thought produced highly paradoxical results. As Zenkovsky wrote, "An individualist to the marrow of his bones . . . he was at the same time Russia's most forceful and brilliant exponent of philosophic impersonalism" (Zenkovsky, 1:386–387). The great paradox of Tolstoy's religious thought, to state it more precisely, is that his Kantian defense of individual autonomy and self-determination culminates in the demise of human personhood, which he denigrates as "animal personality" and sees as a limitation of divine unity. The end or *telos* of individual self-determination, which takes place according to divine reason or logos (recognized by conscience as the moral law), is the loss of self and personhood in logos or, as Tolstoy calls it, "life." This outcome reflects the peculiarity of his notion of "reasonable consciousness": In one respect it functions like Kant's concept of practical reason—the capacity for self-determination according to the ideals of reason, *which capacity for Kant defines personhood*—but in another respect it is radically different, since for Tolstoy the individual self-determination that reasonable consciousness makes possible is merely an instrumental means for the overcoming of personhood, for the ultimate liberation of reasonable consciousness from it. With Kant, by contrast, self-determination explicates what it means to be a person, and neither, of course, is instrumental, since with him personhood is an end-in-itself.

In Kant's conception, self-determination requires a combination of finite and infinite elements: the finite determines itself in accordance with the infinite. Tolstoy follows this as far as his (limited) individualism permits. As we have seen, his faith in the Infinite is achieved through moral (and to a lesser extent cosmological) experience, through self-determination and perfectibility according to the infinite ideals of reason. The clear divergence from Kant comes with his post-conversion religious thought, when the Infinite becomes for Tolstoy the only real value: the finite is radically devalued ("human" becomes "animal") and its "perfectibility" means not so much its true development toward the infinite, i.e., its perfecting in the proper sense of the word, as its self-destruction.

The Kingdom of God Is within You is a tract in which the Kantian "fox" still tries to get a word in. In it we find passages such as: The true life, according to Christ's teaching, "consists in an ever closer approximation to the divine perfection held up before every man, and recognized within himself by every man, in an ever closer and closer approach to the perfect fusion of his will in the will of God" (Tolstoy 1984, 98). These words might be interpreted in the sense of true perfectibility. But soon the spiritualist "hedgehog" speaks with a louder voice, saying that human beings combine in themselves divine and animal natures, and that the animal (which takes the place of an authentically human nature alongside the divine) is to be discarded, not improved:

> Christ's teaching only has power when it demands absolute perfection—that is, the fusion of the divine nature which exists in every man's soul with the will of God—the union of the Son with the Father. Life according to Christ's teaching consists of nothing but this *setting free* of the Son of God, existing in every man, from the animal, and in bringing him closer to the Father. (Tolstoy 1984, 99–100; italics mine)

In another passage the spiritualist hedgehog says that the divine self is "confined in an animal husk" (Tolstoy 1984, 108). All this is a sharp contrast with Kant, for whom perfectibility means the real perfecting of the finite (human) through its ever closer approximation to the infinite (divine). Kant himself was perfectly consistent in his idealism. He argued that since human beings cannot achieve perfection in this life—our will cannot fully coincide with the moral law in a state he calls "holiness"—our process of perfectibility must continue in another life, which is his proof of personal immortality (Kant 1993, 128–129).[50]

Different Conceptions of the Kingdom of God

The religious-philosophical differences between Tolstoy and the Psychological Society idealists came to a head in their respective conceptions of the Kingdom of God. According to Tolstoy, the Kingdom of God is to be achieved through overcoming the human "animal" in what he often calls, misleadingly, self-perfection. He taught that non-resistance to evil is the way to overcome our "animal self" and to achieve the Kingdom of God. The positive content of his ideal is something like the liberation of God, understood as a divine but impersonal spirit of love, from the "animal husk" and more generally from the phenomenal, spatiotemporal universe. With Tolstoy's conception of the Kingdom of God, it is hard to see that the natural and human worlds, or that natural and human history, have any positive purpose.

Most Russian idealists in the Psychological Society (including the spiritualist Lopatin) held a very different idea of the Kingdom of God, one advanced by Vladimir Soloviev in his concept of Godmanhood.[51] The concept is a modern philosophical development of patristic theology, including the Christology of the Council of Chalcedon (the fourth ecumenical council, held in 451), which arrived at the formula that the two distinct natures of Christ, the divine and the human, are united in his person "without division or confusion." This was a remarkably powerful, virtually unprecedented, vindication of the intrinsic worth of humanity: humanity preserves its distinct identity and value even alongside divinity. In this way, Chalcedon can be seen as the beginning of "theological humanism," which is precisely the direction that Soloviev gives it. *Богочеловечество* is a productive term for a profound concept: 1) as the "humanity of God" it conveys the idea of divinity that is also human, intrinsically and not only in the incarnation (the "humanity of God" is further explicated by the ideas of Sophia and *kenosis*); 2) as the "divinity of humanity" it conveys the idea of humanity that is also divine (by origin and vocation); 3) as "divine humanity" it combines the first and second meanings and also suggests the realization of humanity's divine potential or its deification (*theosis*), a mystery which preserves the integrity of humanity even in its deified fulfillment; and 4) as "Godmanhood" it conveys, crucially, the mystery of God and man as ultimately one absolute divine-human being, one pole of which is self-subsistent being (God) and the other is being in the process of becoming and of realizing its divine potential (man).

Throughout his theology of Godmanhood, Soloviev's emphasis is on the value of humanity. In fact, he equates human and divine value, since personhood, divine or human, is of absolute value. It is this divine-human equality that makes Godmanhood possible as a free union between God and man. Without it, the human would be overwhelmed by the divine, preventing the free and autonomous self-realization of human divinity, which is an indispensable component of Godmanhood. It is clear that Godmanhood rests on and describes human perfectibility, the self-realization of our intrinsic divine potential, culminating (transcendently) in theosis and the Kingdom of God. It is also clear that Soloviev's conception of the Kingdom of God is very different than Tolstoy's: it is the *telos* of authentic human perfectibility, our self-realization and development toward the Infinite (God). Indeed, the logic of Soloviev's argument is that God is enriched by our process of perfectibility, so that Godmanhood is throughout (at both poles) a process of infinite perfectibility. (This is the insight of twentieth-century process theology.)

Soloviev's liberal social philosophy flowed naturally from his esteem and hope for humanity: human progress takes place through law and the state, economic life and material culture, science and learning, and art and culture. Similarly, Tolstoy's legal and cultural nihilism flowed naturally from his contempt for humanity: progress consists not in developing our distinctly human capacities and potentials but in casting them aside as impediments to the manifestation of the divine. The comparison of Tolstoy and Soloviev was an inevitable one, of course, for Russian idealist and religious philosophers. It had been done, for example, by some of the contributors to the 1912 volume *On Lev Tolstoy's Religion*. Semyon Frank did not contribute to the volume, despite his influential thesis about Tolstoy's religious individualism, perhaps because he still stood to the side of the "Russian ontologism" or Christian metaphysics of its contributors and publishing house (Путь). In emigration he grew much closer to Soloviev's religious philosophy. In 1949, a year before his death, he wrote that "Solovyov is unquestionably the greatest of Russian philosophers and systematic religious thinkers" (Frank 1950, 9). By then Frank himself had become a leading representative of "Russian religious ontologism."

In 1933 Frank wrote another important essay on Tolstoy, published in Germany (where he lived between 1922 and 1937), "Lev Tolstoy as Thinker and Artist." His earlier essays on Tolstoy had been more admiring than critical (though they were both); this one is more critical than admiring (though it is both). Criticizing Tolstoy from a Solovievian perspective, he argues that his exclusive focus on the absolute or infinite blinds him to the value of the relative, precisely as a means for the progressive realization of the absolute. This makes him a nihilist (Франк 1996b, 466, 471). He does not understand the "great meaning of the Christian idea of 'Godmanhood'" or its valuation of culture, whether in the form of art, science, law, or the state. Culture is the external side of Godmanhood, Frank writes,

> and it presupposes a unity between everyday human life and . . . the divine dignity of human nature. Culture is the effort at forming an ever deeper and more intimate unity in the constant struggle with hard and unyielding empirical material. And even though it, as such, will never reach the ultimate goal of the human spirit—true Godmanhood and, consequently, the embodiment of God in the world—nonetheless it presupposes the reality of mysterious deep inner forces, organically developing and growing, which work on this ultimate goal and strive to impress their reflection on the outermost layer of existence, making it the external symbol of the inner. But for Tolstoy everything external is only the opposition of the inner. (Франк 1996b, 473)

By contrast, for Russian religious ontologism, which Frank had now come to embrace, there is never a complete opposition between divine and mundane reality, but always an inner affinity between them. For it, "the goal is not the overcoming of the world but, on the contrary, its *illumination*, the deification of all that is" (Франк 1996b, 477). Through war, revolution, and exile, it must have been difficult to keep this type of faith in humanity and in the coming of the Kingdom of God. One suspects that it was Soloviev's legacy more than Tolstoy's that helped Frank to sustain it.

(Notes)

1   I am grateful to Caryl Emerson, Gary Hamburg, Gary Jahn, Inessa Medzhibovskaya, and John Randolph for their assistance with this essay.
    This translation appears in Maude, 2:18. See the original in *PSS* 48:195.

2   See Walicki 1979, 332.

3   The first edition was in French (1889); a Russian edition appeared in Switzerland in 1891. See Scanlan 2006, 53.

4   The following overview of the Psychological Society (the next three paragraphs) is drawn from my introduction to Poole 2003, 1–78.

5   An important source on him and the Psychological Society is *Николай Яковлевич Грот в очерках, воспоминаниях и письмах товарищей и учеников, друзей и почитателей*. [abbreviated *GV*]

6   The lecture "О понятии жизни" is reported in the minutes for 14 March 1887, in the archival record at the A. M. Gorky Research Library, Moscow State University. The essay was banned from publication in Russia. "Wishing to make his views public," Maude writes, "Tolstoy read a paper on *Life's Meaning* to the Moscow Psychological Society. The meeting was a crowded one as everybody wished to hear Tolstoy, but Materialism was then rampant, and Tolstoy's treatment of the problem was not generally understood by those who heard his paper" (Maude, 2:229–30). Maude may have exaggerated in writing that the meeting was crowded: according to the archival record, it was in fact a closed session, with twenty-five members present apart from Tolstoy, including Grot. However, Виноградов, 252, describes the meeting as a "public event." In an autobiographical sketch written in 1894, Grot reports that he edited Tolstoy's *On Life*. See *GV*, 341.

7   See Толстой 1892; Толстой 1894; Толстой 1897, continued in Толстой 1898. "Первая ступень" is a plea for vegetarianism.

8   See "Психологическое общество," 457. Five votes were cast against him.

9   Frank seems to be drawing here on *On Life* and on *The Kingdom of God Is within You*. See Tolstoy 1934, chaps. 23–25; and Tolstoy 1984, 104–107. Frank returns to this theme in his 1910 essay "Памяти Льва Толстого." See Франк 1996d.

10 Bulgakov and Berdiaev contributed chapters to *О религии Льва Толстого*. Also see two essays by Bulgakov: Булгаков 1902; and Булгаков 1904 (continued in *Вопросы жизни* 1 (1905): 16–38, and *Вопросы жизни* 3: 1–30). Frank's five main essays on Tolstoy are included in his *Русское мировоззрение*. On Frank's writings, see Medzhibovskaya 2004; and Medzhibovskaya 2005.

11 See Булгаков 1903.

12 See Pipes, 102. Struve wrote a number of articles on Tolstoy, some of which are collected in *Статьи о Льве Толстом* (Sofia, 1921), reprinted in an expanded German version. See Struve.

13 See Scanlan 2006, 52–54; Medzhibovskaya 2008, 275–76.

14 On Grot's philosophical development, see Соколов; specifically on Tolstoy's role, see Шенрок, 42–43.

15 The letter, to Grot's brother Konstantin, is in *GV*, 207-10, here at 208. Tolstoy then launches into a long polemic against academic philosophy and its alleged hostility to religion.

16 Caryl Emerson has argued that what makes Russian literature and criticism so philosophically powerful is, in large part, its understanding and representation of human beings as essentially ideal-positing creatures, and that this understanding spans a wide range of Russian writers and critics. Referring, for example, to Tolstoy, Soloviev, and Bakhtin, she writes that "the point of convergence is their understanding of the creative ideal" and that all three "perceive the highest human relation to be the positing of an ideal" (Emerson 1991, 669). For a more recent, beautifully formulated defense of this thesis, see Emerson 2010. The two novelists discussed in Emerson 2010 are Dostoevsky and Tolstoy, the two critics Bakhtin and Lydia Ginzburg.

17 For the "legal Marxists" as for Grot, ethics was the turning-point. In a review of *Философия и ее общие задачи*, Grot's posthumous collection of articles spanning his positivist and idealist periods, E. V. Spektorsky drew the parallel with *Problems of Idealism*, which included contributions by the four Marxists-turned-idealists, and with Bulgakov's collection, *От марксизма к идеализму*. Spektorsky's review is reprinted in *GV*, 374-86. Spektorsky (1873–1951) was professor (from 1913) and later rector at Kiev University, president of the Philosophical Society there, and an active émigré scholar after the Russian Revolution in the theory of the social sciences, philosophy of law, and philosophy of religion.

18 For the earlier critiques, by D. N. Tsertelev, P. E. Astafiev, and A. A. Kozlov, see Scanlan 2006, 59–64.

19 The essay was also published as a separate brochure (Moscow, 1893). S. L. Frank's essay in *Problems of Idealism* (Frank 2003) also compares Tolstoy and Nietzsche.

20 On its reception, see Scanlan 2006.

21 By the turn of the century, the society had clearly emerged as the theory center of Russian liberalism. Six of its most prominent philosophers (all idealists) were also main theorists of Russian liberalism: B. N. Chicherin (1828–1904), V. S. Soloviev (Solovyov), S. N. Trubetskoy, E. N. Trubetskoy (1863–1920), P. I. Novgorodtsev (1866–1924), and S. A. Kotliarevsky (1873–1939). On them, see Walicki 1987, chapters on Chicherin, Soloviev (Solovyov), and Novgorodtsev; Hamburg 1992; Chicherin; Zimmerman; and Nethercott.

22 Shenrok reproduces Grot's response to *What I Believe* (which Shenrok refers to as "Ma religion"), but does not cite a date or published source.

23 Grot also states this principle in his "Основание нравственного долга," 107–108. See Грот 1892.

24 See my introduction to Poole 2003, 21, 25, 35–42.

25 Tolstoy's "lived idealism" and its role in the development of Russian neo-idealism might be compared to that of the Bakunin family in an earlier cycle of Russian idealism, perhaps especially to the Bakunin women's (Mikhail Aleksandrovich's aunts and sisters) pursuit of self-perfection and moral self-determination and to the faith that ensued from this pursuit. Their practice of "lived idealism" was cultivated by Nikolai Stankevich and his circle, and from there it was embraced by Tolstoy, who revered Stankevich (though he never knew him personally). On the Bakunins and the Stankevich circle, see Randolph. On Stankevich and Tolstoy, see Medzhibovskaya 2008, 23, 64, 110; Orwin, 64–68; and Ginzburg, 49–50.

26 Maude, 1:41, quoting (without clear indication) the conclusion of *Adolescence*; translation modified.

27 Tolstoy 1984, 50–52, 97–108. Also see the "Afterword to *The Kreutzer Sonata*," where Tolstoy distinguishes between two types of moral guidance, following external rules or pursuing an "unattainable perfection": "A man who professes an external law is like someone standing in the light of a lantern fixed to a post. It is light all around him, but there is nowhere further for him to walk. A man who professes the teaching of Christ is like a man carrying a lantern before him on a long, or not so long, pole: the light is in front of him . . . always encouraging him to walk further" (Tolstoy 1987b, 69). On Tolstoy's theology of perfection, see Gustafson, 427–441.

28 Dostoevsky also saw Kant as relevant to the existential dilemma he posed in his works, "what if there is no God and no immortality of the soul?" Many others did too. "In Dostoevsky's age," according to Paperno, "Kant's antinomies of pure reason became topical" (Paperno, 125). On their importance for Dostoevsky, see also Scanlan 2002; Cassedy; and Knapp.

29 He did so in letters to A. A. Fet of 30 January 1873 and 29 April 1876. See *PSS* 62:6–7, 271–72; Maude, 1:335–36, 360 (who seems to misdate the first letter as 30 January 1872); and Medzhibovskaya 2008, 138, 154.

30 See the discussion of Frank's "religious individualism" in Swoboda's excellent study, 562–93. Swoboda cites Frank's article "Лев Толстой и русская интеллигенция," but otherwise does not refer to Tolstoy (Swoboda, 582–583).

31 Maude's notion of a "moral universe" combines the moral and cosmological modes of experiencing the infinite that I distinguished above.

32 According to Ivanov-Razumnik, the journal "played a large role in the history of the revival of philosophic thought in Russia. Perhaps it received its special importance because it was not the organ of one or another philosophical group but was, on the contrary, nonpartisan in the philosophic sense. True, the directors of this journal and the large part of its continuous contributors quite definitely adhered to 'idealism' in one or another of its aspects; but at the same time the pages of the journal were always open to the most 'realistic' doctrines and to lively exchange of opinions among opposing philosophic views. . . . Readers thus had before them a kind of 'parliament of philosophic opinions'" (Иванов-Разумник, 452).

33 See the classic account of them as liberal philosophers in Walicki 1987, chaps. 2–3.

34 See his essay, "Contemporary Tasks of Russian Life," written in the summer of 1855.

35 See В. С. Соловьев, *Чтения о Богочеловечестве*, in Соловьев, 3:1–181; Критика отвлеченных начал, in Соловьев, 2:v–xvi; 1–397.

36 See my essay Poole 2012.

37 Walicki puts them at opposite poles of Russian religious thought, referring to Konstantin Mochulsky's remark (in his 1951 book Владимир Соловьев. *Жизнь и учение*) that the two men were almost physically incapable of breathing the same air (Walicki 1979, 335). On their relations, see also Лосев, 499–506. Soloviev's last work, *Three Conversations on War, Progress and the End of World History, with a Short Story of the Anti-Christ* (1899), is a merciless polemic against Tolstoyanism, as represented by the (extremely negative) character of the prince. For compelling readings of this work, see Kornblatt; and Valliere. Kolstø has recently argued that Soloviev casts the prince, and by implication Tolstoy, as the servant of the devil. See Kolstø, esp. 318–21. More generally, see Hooper.

38 One of the many places where Soloviev specifies his view that true faith cannot be coerced but rests on "the evidence of things not seen" (Hebrews 11:1) is his essay "The Jews and the Christian Problem" (1884), which is translated in part in Frank 1950, 112.

39 See Poole 2010a, which focuses on Medzhibovskaya 2008.

40 Such as *Religion within the Boundaries of Mere Reason*. Upon reading it in 1905, Tolstoy wrote that "Kant is very close to me" and "I am intensely in awe of him" (Jahn, 63).

41 In the *Groundwork of the Metaphysic of Morals*, see chap. 1 on the good will, duty, and the moral law, and in chap. 2 the section on "Autonomy of the Will as the supreme principle of morality." See Kant 1964, 61–73, 108.

42 I have explored this topic in the following essays: Poole 1999; Poole 2010b; and Poole 2008a (conference materials available on-line at the conference website).

43 See Walicki 1987, chap. 2, esp. 160-61; Hamburg 2010; and Poole 2008a.

44 See Scanlan 2010; and my articles on three Russian panpsychists for the *Routledge Encyclopedia of Philosophy* (online edition, 2002): Sergei Askoldov, Aleksei Kozlov, and Lev Lopatin.

45 For good statements of his spiritualistic metaphysics, see his essays Лопатин 1912b; and Лопатин 1917.

46 Lopatin first expounded his philosophy in his book *Область умозрительных вопросов* (1886), the first volume of his *Положительные задачи философии* (see Лопатин 1886). The second volume is *Закон причинной связи, как основа умозрительного знания действительности* (1891). It is possible that Tolstoy read the first volume as he was writing *On Life*. In the mid and late-1880s he occasionally conversed and dined with Lopatin, as he indicates in his diary (*PSS*

49:64, 74, 90; *PSS* 50:20–21). On 13 April 1889 he records that he read a paper by Lopatin on freedom of the will (*PSS* 50:66). No doubt the paper was "Условия свободной самодеятельности человека," which Lopatin presented before a meeting of the Psychological Society on 3 April 1889 and which forms the first part of his short book (100 pp.) published later that year, Лопатин 1889.

47 Scanlan 2010 deals carefully with the issue of personalism among Kozlov, Lopatin, and Lossky, making the necessary qualifications and distinctions.

48 See Scanlan 2006, 60–64, for an excellent analysis of these critiques.

49 See Zenkovsky, 1:391, 393–94; Walicki 1979, 331–34.

50 Scanlan indicates that there is a "curious contrast" between Kant and Tolstoy on this point, with Tolstoy maintaining that perfectibility ceases at death, even if the self survives it (Scanlan 2006, 58). Whether Tolstoy defended personal immortality remains a matter of controversy among scholars. The overall direction of his post-conversion position argues against it: what is immortal is the infinite (God) within us. This is Zenkovsky's argument in Зеньковский, 53–54. In *What I Believe* (1884), chap. 8, Tolstoy writes at length and unambiguously against the idea of personal immortality, including the following lines: "I can no longer doubt that my personal life perishes, but the life of the whole world according to the will of the Father does not perish, and only merging with it gives me the possibility of salvation. But this so little in comparison with exalted religious beliefs in a personal future! Though it is little, it is correct" (*PSS* 23:400). Maude offers the following good overall assessment of his views of the afterlife: "he refrained from assertions as to the kind of existence that will succeed the death of our bodies," including "[w]hether there be a personal immortality" or "whether we shall merge into the Infinite as rain-drops fall into the ocean. . . . For whatever the future may have in store, we shall best prepare for it by helping to establish the Kingdom of God on earth" (Maude, 2:40). However, Maude later suggests (less plausibly, in my view) that by the time of *On Life* Tolstoy had come to believe in a future life in the sense of personal immortality (Maude, 2:229).

51 The following discussion is based on my articles, which provide documentation: Poole 2010b; Poole 2007; and Poole 2008b.

Works Cited:

Berdiaev, N. A. "The Ethical Problem in the Light of Philosophical Idealism." *Problems of Idealism: Essays in Russian Social Philosophy*. Ed. Randall Poole. New Haven: Yale UP, 2003: 161–97

Berlin, Isaiah. "The Hedgehog and the Fox." *Russian Thinkers*. Ed. Henry Hardy and Aileen Kelly. New York: Penguin Books, 1994: 22–81

Bulgakov, S. N. (Булгаков, С. Н.) "Basic Problems of the Theory of Progress." *Problems of Idealism: Essays in Russian Social Philosophy*. Ed. Randall Poole. New Haven: Yale UP, 2003: 85–123

---. "Карлейль и Толстой." *Новый путь* 12 (1904): 227–60

---. "Л. Н. Толстой." *О религии Льва Толстого*. Под ред. С. Н. Булгакова. Москва: Путь, 1912: 1–26

---, ред. *О религии Льва Толстого*. Москва: Путь, 1912

---. *От марксизма к идеализму. Сборник статей (1896–1903)*. Санкт-Петербург: Издательство Товарищества "Общественная польза," 1903

---. "Васнецов, Достоевский, Вл. Соловьев, Толстой (параллели)." *Литературное дело*. Санкт-Петербург, 1902: 119–39

Cassedy, Steven. *Dostoevsky's Religion*. Stanford: Stanford UP, 2005

Chicherin, B. N. (Чичерин, Б.Н.) *Liberty, Equality, and the Market: Essays by B. N. Chicherin*. Ed. and tr. G. M. Hamburg. New Haven: Yale UP, 1998

---. *Наука и религия*. 2-е изд. Москва: Типолитография товарищества И. Н. Кушнерев, 1901

Emerson, Caryl. "On Persons as Open-Ended Ends-in-Themselves (The View from Two Novelists and Two Critics)." *A History of Russian Philosophy, 1830–1930: Faith, Reason, and the Defense of Human Dignity*. Ed. G. M. Hamburg and Randall A. Poole. Cambridge: Cambridge UP, 2010: 381–90

---. "Solov'ev, the Late Tolstoi, and the Early Bakhtin on the Problem of Shame and Love." *Slavic Review* 50:3 (Fall 1991): 663–71

Frank, S. L. (Франк, С.Л.) "The Ethic of Nihilism: A Characterization of the Russian Intelligentsia's Moral Outlook." *Vekhi/Landmarks: A Collection of Articles about the Russian Intelligentsia*. Ed. and tr. Marshall S. Shatz and Judith E. Zimmerman. Armonk, NY: M. E. Sharpe, 1994: 131–55

---. "Friedrich Nietzsche and the Ethics of 'Love of the Distant.'" *Problems of Idealism: Essays in Russian Social Philosophy*. Ed. Randall Poole. New Haven: Yale UP, 2003: 198–241

---. "Лев Толстой и русская интеллигенция." С. Л. Франк. *Русское мировоззрение*. Санкт-Петербург: Наука, 1996: 440–444 [abbreviated as Франк 1996a]

---. "Лев Толстой как мыслитель и художник." С. Л. Франк. *Русское мировоззрение*. Санкт-Петербург: Наука, 1996: 459–478 [abbreviated as Франк 1996b]

---. "Нравственное учение Л. Н. Толстого (К 80-летнему юбилею Толстого 28 августа 1908 г.).” С. Л. Франк. *Русское мировоззрение.* Санкт-Петербург: Наука, 1996: 432–439 [abbreviated as Франк 1996с]

---. “Памяти Льва Толстого.” С. Л. Франк. *Русское мировоззрение.* Санкт-Петербург: Наука, 1996: 445–455 [abbreviated as Франк 1996d]

---. ed. *A Solovyov Anthology.* Tr. Natalie Duddington. London: SCM Press, 1950

Ginzburg, Lydia. *On Psychological Prose.* Tr. and ed. Judson Rosengrant. Princeton: Princeton University Press, 1991

Грот, Н. Я. “Нравственные идеалы нашего времени (Фридрих Ницше и Лев Толстой).” *Вопросы философии и психологии* 16 (1893): 129–54

---. “О задачах журнала.” *Вопросы философии и психологии* 1 (1889): v–xx

---. “Основание нравственного долга.” *Вопросы философии и психологии* 15 (1892): 71–114

---. “От редакции.” *Вопросы философии и психологии* 3 (1890): v–vii

Gustafson, Richard F. *Leo Tolstoy, Resident and Stranger: A Study in Fiction and Theology.* Princeton: Princeton UP, 1986

Hamburg, G. M. *Boris Chicherin and Early Russian Liberalism, 1828–1866.* Stanford: Stanford UP, 1992

---. “Boris Chicherin and Human Dignity in History.” *A History of Russian Philosophy, 1830–1930: Faith, Reason, and the Defense of Human Dignity.* Ed. G. M. Hamburg and Randall A. Poole. Cambridge: Cambridge UP, 2010: 111–130

Hooper, Cynthia. “Forms of Love: Vladimir Solov’ev and Lev Tolstoy on Eros and Ego.” *Russian Review* 60:3 (July 2001): 360–80

Иванов-Разумник, Р. В. *История русской общественной мысли.* 2-е изд. В 2-х томах. Санкт-Петербург, 1908

Jahn, Gary R. “Tolstoj and Kant.” *New Perspectives on Nineteenth-Century Russian Prose.* Ed. George J. Gutsche and Lauren G. Leighton. Columbus, OH: Slavica Publishers, 1981: 60-70

Kant, Immanuel, *Critique of Practical Reason.* Tr. Lewis White Beck. 3rd ed. New York: Macmillan, 1993

---. *Groundwork of the Metaphysic of Morals.* Tr. H. J. Paton. New York: Harper & Row, 1964

Кизеветтер, А. А. *На рубеже двух столетий. Воспоминания, 1881–1914.* Прага: Орбис, 1929; Newtonville, MA, 1974

Knapp, Liza. *The Annihilation of Inertia: Dostoevsky and Metaphysics.* Evanston, IL: Northwestern University Press, 1996

Kolstø, Pål. “The Demonized Double: The Image of Lev Tolstoi in Russian Orthodox Polemics.” *Slavic Review* 65:2 (Summer 2006): 304–24

Kornblatt, Judith. “Soloviev on Salvation: The Story of the ‘Short Story of the Antichrist.’” *Russian Religious Thought.* Ed. Judith Deutsch Kornblatt and Richard F. Gustafson. Madison, WI: University of Wisconsin Press, 1996: 68–87

Lopatin L.M. (Лопатин, Л. М.) “Две отчетные речи Л. М. Лопатина.” *Вопросы философии и психологии* 111 (1912): 181–211 [abbreviated as Лопатин 1912a]

---. *Философские характеристики и речи*. Москва: Путь, 1911

---. "From the Moscow Psychological Society." *Problems of Idealism: Essays in Russian Social Philosophy*. Ed. Randall Poole. New Haven: Yale UP, 2003: 79–80

---. "Неотложные задачи современной мысли." *Вопросы философии и психологии* 136 (1917): 1–80

---. *Положительные задачи философии*. В 2-ч частях. Москва, 1886–1891

---. "Спиритуализм как монистическая система философии." *Вопросы философии и психологии* 115 (1912): 435–471 [abbreviated as Лопатин 1912b]

---. "Теоретические основы сознательной нравственной жизни." *Вопросы философии и психологии* 5 (1890): 34–83

---. *Вопрос о свободе воли*. Москва, 1889

Лосев, А. Ф. *Владимир Соловьев и его время*. Москва: Прогресс, 1990

Maude, Aylmer. *The Life of Tolstoy*, 2 vols. Oxford: Oxford UP, 1987

Medzhibovskaya, Inessa. "Dogmatism or Moral Logic? Simon Frank Confronts Tolstoy's Ethical Thought (1902–1909)." *Tolstoy Studies Journal* 16 (2004): 18–32

---. "Simon Frank Confronts Tolstoy's Ethical Thought (The Later Years)." *Tolstoy Studies Journal* 17 (2005): 43–58

---. *Tolstoy and the Religious Culture of His Time: A Biography of a Long Conversion, 1845–1887*. Lanham, MD: Lexington Books, 2008

Nethercott, Frances. "Russian Liberalism and the Philosophy of Law." *A History of Russian Philosophy, 1830–1930: Faith, Reason, and the Defense of Human Dignity*. Ed. G.M. Hamburg and Randall A. Poole. Cambridge: Cambridge UP, 2010, 248–65

Николай Яковлевич Грот в очерках, воспоминаниях и письмах товарищей и учеников, друзей и почитателей. Санкт-Петербург: Типография Министерства Путей Сообщения, 1911 [abbreviated *GV*]

Orwin, Donna. *Tolstoy's Art and Thought, 1847–1880*. Princeton: Princeton UP, 1993

Paperno, Irina. *Suicide as a Cultural Institution in Dostoevsky's Russia*. Ithaca, NY: Cornell UP, 1997

Pipes, Richard. *Struve: Liberal on the Right, 1905–1944*. Cambridge, MA: Harvard UP, 1980

Poole, Randall. "The Greatness of Vladimir Soloviev: A Review Essay," *Canadian Slavonic Papers/Revue canadienne des slavistes* 50:1–2 (March-June 2008): 201–223 [abbreviated as Poole 2008b]

---. "Human Dignity and the Kingdom of God: A Russian Theological Perspective (Vladimir Soloviev)." *Listening/Journal of Religion and Culture* 42:3 (Fall 2007): 33–54

---. "Kantian Foundations of Russian Liberal Theory: Human Dignity, Justice, and the Rule of Law." *The Weimar Moment: Liberalism, Political Theology, and*

Law. Institute for Legal Studies, University of Wisconsin Law School, 2008 [abbreviated as Poole 2008a].

---. "The Neo-Idealist Reception of Kant in the Moscow Psychological Society," *Journal of the History of Ideas* 60:2 (April 1999): 319–343

---, ed. *Problems of Idealism: Essays in Russian Social Philosophy*. Foreword by Caryl Emerson. New Haven: Yale UP, 2003

---. "Religious Toleration, Freedom of Conscience, and Russian Liberalism." *Kritika: Explorations in Russian and Eurasian History* 13:3 (Summer 2012): 611–634

---. "'Russia's First Modern Man': Tolstoy, Kant, and Russian Religious Thought." *Tolstoy Studies Journal* 22 (2010): 99–117 [abbreviated as Poole 2010a]

---. "Vladimir Soloviev's Philosophical Anthropology: Autonomy, Dignity, Perfectibility." *A History of Russian Philosophy, 1830–1930: Faith, Reason, and the Defense of Human Dignity*. Ed. G. M. Hamburg and Randall A. Poole. Cambridge: Cambridge UP, 2010: 131–149 [abbreviated as Poole 2010b]

"Психологическое общество." *Вопросы философии и психологии* 23 (1894): 455–74

Pyman, Avril. *Pavel Florensky: A Quiet Genius. The Tragic and Extraordinary Life of Russia's Unknown da Vinci*. New York: Continuum, 2010

Randolph, John. *The House in the Garden: The Bakunin Family and the Romance of Russian Idealism*. Ithaca, NY: Cornell UP, 2007

Scanlan, James P. *Dostoevsky the Thinker*. Ithaca, NY: Cornell UP, 2002

---. "Russian Panpsychism: Kozlov, Lopatin, Losskii." *A History of Russian Philosophy, 1830–1930: Faith, Reason, and the Defense of Human Dignity*. Ed. G. M. Hamburg and Randall A. Poole. Cambridge: Cambridge UP, 2010: 150–68

---. "Tolstoy among the Philosophers: His Book *On Life* and Its Critical Reception." *Tolstoy Studies Journal* 18 (2006): 52–69

Шенрок, В. И. "К биографии Н. Я. Грота (1852–1899)." *Николай Яковлевич Грот в очерках, воспоминаниях и письмах товарищей и учеников, друзей и почитателей*. Санкт-Петербург: Типография Министерства Путей Сообщения, 1911: 1–56

Соколов, П. П. "Философские взгляды и научная деятельность Н. Я. Грота." Н. Я. Грот. *Философия и ее общие задачи*. Сборник статей. Санкт-Петербург: Типография А. С. Суворина, 1904: lxvii–civ

Soloviev, V.S. (Solovyov, V.S.; Соловьев. В.С.) *Lectures on Divine Humanity*. Tr. Peter P. Zouboff. Rev. and ed. Boris Jakim. Hudson, NY: Lindisfarne Press, 1995

---. *Собрание сочинений Владимира Соловьева*. Под ред. С. М. Соловьева и Э. Л. Радлова. 2-е изд. В 10-ти томах. Санкт-Петербург: Книгоиздательское товарищество "Просвещение," 1911–1914

Struve, P. B. "Leo Tolstoj." *Jahrbücher für Kultur und Geschichte der Slaven*, 9:1–2 (1933): 5–36

Swoboda, Philip J. *The Philosophical Thought of S. L. Frank, 1902–1915: A Study of the Metaphysical Impulse in Early Twentieth-Century Russia*. Columbia University, PhD dissertation, 1992

Tolstoy, Leo. (Толстой, Л.Н.) ---. "Что такое искусство?" *Вопросы философии и психологии* 40 (1897): 979–1027

---. "Что такое искусство? (Окончание)." *Вопросы философии и психологии* 41 (1898): 5–137

---. *A Confession and Other Religious Writings.* Tr. Jane Kentish. New York: Penguin Books, 1987 [abbreviated as Tolstoy 1987a]

---. "К вопросу о свободе воли." *Вопросы философии и психологии* 21 (1894): 1–7

---. *The Kingdom of God Is within You: Christianity Not as a Mystic Religion but as a New Theory of Life.* Tr. Constance Garnett. Lincoln, NE: University of Nebraska Press, 1984

---. *The Lion and the Honeycomb: The Religious Writings of Tolstoy.* Tr. Richard Chandler. Ed. A. N. Wilson. New York: Harper and Row, 1987 [abbreviated as Tolstoy 1987b]

---. *On Life and Essays on Religion.* Tr. Aylmer Maude. Oxford: Oxford UP, 1934

---. "Первая ступень." *Вопросы философии и психологии* 13 (1892): 109–44

---. (*PSS*) *Полное собрание сочинений в 90 томах, академическое юбилейное издание.* Москва: Государственное издательство художественной литературы, 1928–58

Трубецкой, Е. Н. *Смысл жизни.* Берлин: Книгоиздательство "Слово," 1922

Valliere, Paul. *Modern Russian Theology. Bukharev, Soloviev, Bulgakov. Orthodox Theology in a New Key.* Grand Rapids, MI: William B. Eerdmans Publishing Company, 2000: 205–223

Виноградов, Н. Д. "Краткий исторический очерк деятельности Московского Психологического Общества за 25 лет." *Вопросы философии и психологии* 103 (1910): 249–262

Walicki, Andrzej. *A History of Russian Thought from the Enlightenment to Marxism.* Tr. Hilda Andrews-Rusiecka. Stanford: Stanford UP, 1979

---. *Legal Philosophies of Russian Liberalism.* Oxford: Clarendon Press, 1987

Zenkovsky, V. V. (Зеньковский, В. В.) *A History of Russian Philosophy.* Tr. George L. Kline. 2 vols. New York: Columbia UP, 1953.

---. "Проблема бессмертия у Л. Н. Толстого." *О религии Льва Толстого.* Под ред. С. Н. Булгакова. Москва: Путь, 1912: 27–58

Zimmerman, Judith E. "Russian Liberal Theory, 1900–1917." *Canadian-American Slavic Studies* 14:1 (Spring 1980): 1–20

The End of *On Life*: Kant with Tolstoy

Jeff Love
Clemson University

We can protect ourselves against other things, but when it comes to death all men live in a city without walls.

— Epicurus

We must return to the end for the sake of which we live, the *hou heneka*, in Aristotle's language. If we observe science from this perspective, the perspective of the end, we shall quickly see that science is unable to determine the end for which we live. Science is blind in this sense because it serves an end that it does not set for itself: preservation of the "animal personality"—self-preservation—and nothing more. Science has in effect thrown ends out because it is in thrall to a single end: bodily immortality, the sole good, a kind of well-being or, referring once again to Aristotle, *eudaimonia*, which Tolstoy describes as *благо*. This is the negative moment of turning to the end for which we live because we discover that the striving for that end cannot achieve what it purports to achieve. According to Tolstoy, mere self-preservation cannot achieve the good it covets, cannot cheat death, but rather is a form of death itself. There is of course a corresponding positive moment of turning to the end. The precondition for understanding this positive moment: the conclusion that self-preservation is a vain and misleading enterprise. Recognition of the vanity of self-preservation begins the turn to what is truly human, reason, or as Tolstoy calls it, "rational consciousness" (*разумное сознание*).[1] Rational consciousness is, for all that, not the way of despair; it does not force one to assume a soberly pessimistic view of human striving. To the contrary, rational consciousness turns us towards the only way of hope, the only way of living a human life, defined here as living for the sake of that which is not condemned to die, rationality itself. Rational consciousness is the same everywhere, establishing the unity of equality, the supreme бла́го. Forget the body, the particular, the rhetoric of "bodies and languages," and take up the universal, the law of reason, genuine well-being—this is the slogan lurking within the relentless repetitions of Tolstoy's *On Life*.

Thus, I begin this essay with a summary, an end of sorts, an approach characteristic of Tolstoy's treatise in which the many shifts from synoptic figuration (one has to think only of the figure of the miller introduced on the first pages of the treatise) to particular chains of thought are remarkable. Tolstoy develops a mode of discourse that is in fact constantly negotiating between holistic overview and atomistic particular as the argument moves through its various stages. One might insist that this structuring tactic serves the purposes of clarity above all, and leave the matter at that. But this is surely rather short-sighted. For the concern about the relation between the general and the particular is one of the focal points of the treatise; it reveals Tolstoy's peculiar affinity with the German tradition of thought that starts with Leibniz but takes definitive form in the works of the one great philosopher cited in the epigraph to *On Life*, Immanuel Kant.[2]

What this affinity might amount to remains a question with intriguing consequences for interpretation of the treatise and its attitude to philosophy. Hence, I propose to explore Kantian echoes in Tolstoy's treatise primarily as a means of teasing out a particular interpretation and not in order to establish, as is the wont of much traditional criticism, a genetic link or trail of influence. In my view, the latter approach is most frequently based on a decidedly reductive view of influence, as if one author merely grafts on to his/her work that of another as seen by a third, the interpreter. Aside from that objection, one has to wonder why it would be important, or necessary, to impose a generalizing influence narrative on the works of a particular author. In any case, it is doubtful that such a narrative would do justice to Tolstoy. We might end up succumbing to the same temptations as his contemporaries who denied him originality as a thinker because they read so many influences into his treatises. And, if Tolstoy's epigraphs invite this approach, one could argue that they do so with an irony not always available to his critics.

With these cautions in mind, I shall proceed below first by examining the Kantian echoes in Tolstoy as they coalesce around the relation of general and particular that is so important in the treatise. I shall then return to the issue of influence to address one of the crucial motivations of the treatise, to reconcile what Heidegger referred to as three fundamental ways of apprehending the whole: philosophy, literature and religion.[3] To my mind, it is the treatise's attempt, as often striking as subtle, at reconciling these disparate discourses that gives us access to its genuine originality (though indebted to Rousseau), and, perhaps, to its genuine failure as well.[4]

I.

As the epigraph might suggest, Kant's presence in *On Life* is elusive, indirect.[5] Yet, the first steps of the argument Tolstoy makes in the treatise deal with a distinctively Kantian concern: the relation of facts and values.[6] Before delving into Tolstoy's inflection of this relation in the treatise, let me provide a very simplified sketch of several key aspects of it so that my presuppositions are clear.

The relation between facts and values is one between the "is" and the "ought," and it assumes (perhaps precariously) that this latter distinction has ontological credibility. What does the relation suggest? For one thing, it suggests that there is a vast realm freed of value in which things are without the admixture of human evaluation (or manipulation). A reed is, for example. One cannot simply say that to declare the existence of this reed is to make a value judgment, or so it would seem. Yet, that one ought to protect the reed is another matter. In this case, an important concern of value, say, that reeds should not be cut down because to do so is to commit violence against a natural object, comes to the fore.

If we look a bit more closely, we see that an ontological determination of fact, that the reed is, precedes another kind of determination as to how to deal with the reed's being. The "is" grounds the "ought," the reed is knowable firmly as fact, the ought is more questionable. Facts provide the basis for values, and they do so only insofar as they are not values; and, significantly, if facts are necessary as a basis for valuation, there is otherwise no necessary connection between a given fact and the value judgment applied to it. Value judgments are creatures of possibility not necessity.

This distinction between what is and what may or may not be is fundamental to the facts and values relation. This is, in other words, a modal distinction that classifies things according to whether their being is invariable or not. A fact is, if it is, always in the same way. But a value, if it is, may be radically variable. Between theory and practice, necessity and possibility, or necessity and freedom, there is a fundamental distinction: one cannot alter what is, if it is, but one can alter those things which may or may not be, whose being includes the possibility of their being other.

What is at issue here? Authority, and specifically the authority that resides in fact or value. The dominant view we still take for granted is that facts are at least in principle determinable by means having nothing to do with an underlying valuation: a green truck is a green truck here as elsewhere in the world.[7] The implication of course is that valuation is not so determinable, that valuation differs in different circumstances, and, hence, that value is much more malleable and elusive than fact. Put more simply, facts partake of necessity, the bedrock of objectivity, whereas values do not; they are variable, always possibly other.

The irony in this, lost neither on Kant nor on Tolstoy, is the implicit valorization of stasis over variability as providing a more suitable model for authority. Fact has accordingly greater authority than value because it can be determined once and for all; fact emerges as the venue of the general, whereas value is inevitably particular, contingent—and unpredictable, a creation of historical circumstance.

II.

This hierarchy is precisely what Tolstoy seeks to reverse in the treatise while retaining the other hierarchy, that of being over becoming, on which it is based. In doing so, Tolstoy presents the obverse of the picture given above, at least on the surface. Moreover, he does so through an interesting critique of scientific inquiry that looks back to Rousseau and forward to Heidegger and, of course, Max Weber.[8] I want to linger a while on this critique, which is crucial to the treatise as a whole as well as to its peculiarly Kantian aspect.

The argument is quite radical. Tolstoy attacks the possibility of properly ascertaining facts without some concept of value. Specifically, Tolstoy brings into question an object. He wants to know how one can determine which properties determine the identity of any given object. He puts this question based on a fascinating, dogmatic assumption: "every object has as many aspects as there are radii in a sphere, that is to say, an infinite number, and it is impossible to study all the sides" ["у всякого предмета столько же сторон, сколько радиусов в шаре, т. е. без числа, и что нельзя изучать со всех сторон"] (*OLMT,* 12/*PSS* 26:321).[9]

The infinite, here as elsewhere, plays a central role in Tolstoyan thinking.[10] If one accepts Tolstoy's mathematical analogy, then objects essentially dissolve in themselves and into each other. Definition is precisely that, a de-fining, or imposition of limits on, an essentially indefinable or infinite multiplicity. Hence, the question must arise as to which criteria permit authoritative definition: otherwise, there would be no objects. What a remarkable point this is! Without a principle of selection, which cannot be immanent in the objects themselves—for what is immanent in them exceeds all definition—there can be no objects.

What should not be missed here is the idealism inherent in Tolstoy's argument. The ostensibly dogmatic assumption of the infinity of objects is idealist to the core: it equates what is with mathematics, not a terribly unusual equation and, indeed, one that has become explicit in the equation of mathematics and ontology made by a leading contemporary philosopher, Alain Badiou (Badiou. 1–20).

Yet, Tolstoy shows his hand in this argument since the senses cannot perceive the infinite, the infinite does not make itself available for everyday observation: just try to visualize a chiliagon or an object from all possible perspectives at once, and this difficulty will become quite apparent. Now, Tolstoy's fundamentally idealist stance compels him to condemn any one view purporting to convey a full knowledge of things, a kind of knowledge that is, presumably, free of presuppositions or other determinative conditions. In a complicated way, for Tolstoy there are no facts, just interpretations.

Let me explain this point more carefully. It is quite clear that, if an object is "an" infinite multiplicity, no one description of that object can purport to contain all descriptions of it; and, thus, no one description of the object can claim not to be derived from a particular way of perceiving the object. This way, a relation to the object (what Tolstoy will refer to in the treatise as a "relation to the world"), determines that object with an awareness, however, that that determination is not complete but allows for still other determinations, which must provide a different object. The importance of the relation is that it denies immediate access to the object at the same time as it grants access to it. There is no way beyond limitation, no object in itself or for the divine mind. Thus, relation is determinative of the "is," of what might constitute a fact, and in what might consist the conditionality of that fact.

What, then, determines this determinative relation? This is where the three discourses come into the fray: religion, literature and philosophy. Yet, it is somewhat too soon to proceed to this part of our discussion. For the moment, I should like to investigate Tolstoy's response to this particular question. Only after I have set out the two levels of Tolstoy's response, shall I be in a position to point out the affinity with Kant and the peculiar significance of that affinity.

Tolstoy's response is to claim that reason is the determining (and generalizing) authority. This is certainly the most brazenly philosophical aspect of *On Life*, a somewhat peculiar one, to be sure. Philosophy is the sovereign—hence, idealist—discourse of reason, and one should not confuse philosophy with discourses of revelation (religion) or myth (literature). A narrative philosophy becomes literature, and religious philosophy is, in the words of Martin Heidegger, a "round square" (Heidegger, 8).

Tolstoy is more sensitive to the competition with literature than with religion. He is eager to indicate that reason's authority arises from its not being conditioned by time; in other words, for Tolstoy, reason is not historical. Tolstoy is by no means a historicist, and philosophy does not reveal itself through narrative means, perhaps a surprising conclusion to draw in regard to Tolstoy given his status as a profoundly philosophical novelist. To the contrary, Tolstoy is far more eager to align philosophy with religion as evinced by one of the most interesting chapters in *On Life*.

This is chapter XVII, entitled "Birth by the spirit," which opens with an astonishing declaration: "'Ye must be born again,' said Jesus. This does not mean that someone commands man to be born again, but that he is inevitably brought to it. To have life he must be reborn to the life of rational consciousness" ["'Должно вам родиться снова,' сказал Христос. Не то чтобы человеку кто-нибудь велел родиться, но человек неизбежно приведен к этому. Чтобы иметь жизнь, ему нужно вновь родиться в этом существовании—разумным сознанием"] (*OLMT,* 72/*PSS* 26:367).

Tolstoy equates life with freedom and freedom with rationality. This is Tolstoy's greatest affinity with Kant. But is the affinity anything more than superficial? The basic question here, a momentous one, is, then, not only whether there is some similarity between Kant and Tolstoy regarding the role they ascribe to reason as being an agent of freedom, but also whether that similarity has any depth; that is, whether that similarity in fact extends to the concept of reason itself.

III.

It would be foolhardy to claim that Tolstoy's thinking about the nature of reason is in any way comparable to that of Kant in terms of its complexity, range and evocativeness. But this could be said for many of those who learned from Kant. Besides, it is a more or less standard cliché of the sorts of apologetics which come out from under Kant's shadow. Let us not repeat them.

The affinity concerning the role of reason is, however striking. I shall employ one of the primary Kantian oppositions, crucial to Kant's practical philosophy, his philosophy of freedom, to explain it further: that of heteronomy and autonomy. From the perspective of freedom, heteronomy describes a form of enslavement to impulse, to the sensory stimuli of the world as it is. One who is acting heteronomously is reacting, more or less instinctively, without reflecting on that action as such. To put this in a way taken up in a different context by a different thinker, reactivity is a form of slavery to one's environment: one is continuously defined by what one encounters.[11] Autonomy describes a very different attitude to one's environment. To act autonomously is to choose deliberately, to decide to respond in certain ways to a set of stimuli or, indeed, to change that response or the stimuli themselves.

An instructive variant of this distinction is provided by Robert Brandom's very Kantian distinction between sentience and sapience. Brandom writes:

> Picking us out by our capacity for reason and understanding expresses a commitment to take *sapience*, rather than *sentience* as the constellation of characteristics that distinguishes us. Sentience is what we share with non-verbal animals such as cats—the capacity to be *aware* in the sense of being *awake*. Sentience, which so far as our understanding yet reaches is an exclusively biological phenomenon, is in turn to be distinguished from the mere reliable differential responsiveness we sentients share with artifacts such as thermostats and land mines. Sapience concerns understanding or intelligence, rather than irritability or arousal. One is treating something as sapient insofar as one explains its behavior by attributing to it intentional states such as belief and desire as constituting reasons for that behavior. (Brandom, 5)

Brandom brings out nicely the difference between automatic and reflective response; only the latter constitutes sapience and it does so because the response may vary. That is the whole point of sapience, that response is not mandated to be the same every time: the animal is condemned to repeat, but the sapient being is not—variation is the by-word of sapience.

If we adapt this to our previous discussions, we come to an intriguing result. Tolstoy's attack on science, on the "is," is an attack on the animal obedience it imposes. The "is," objectivity, requires a purely passive, reactive approach. That is the point of objectivity, after all, to take things out of our control so that we no longer need think about how we might deal with them. Objectivity undermines freedom. And, since freedom is the essence of life, something Tolstoy never tires of repeating, it is but a short step to the proposition that objectification is a sort of death or terminal point, what one might refer to, using another terminology, as reification. To return to the opening paragraph of this essay, the significance of Tolstoy's equation of self-preservation with death might become clearer. If we take life to be the highest expression of freedom, and death to be its opposite, then it is no great matter to claim that the striving of science to objectify all things, including our lives, is indeed a striving to die by becoming automata, mere sentients.

Let me draw a few strands of discussion together here. The central claim is that science, in pursuit of self-preservation, ends up turning all things into objects. This is by no means an obvious equation. But science demands predictability; freedom is anathema. The cost of pursuing science in support of self-preservation is that of making things calculable and predictable. Nothing unexpected can occur. In other words, the pursuit of self-preservation returns us to the state of the animal: science substitutes predictable reactivity for the instinct that we are lacking and fills in that gap. In doing so, however, it also robs us of freedom. Tolstoy explicitly connects the pursuit of science in this fashion with the "animal personality"; and, indeed, it is the singular prerogative of the animal personality to function as a part of an environment, though, in human beings, it may not appear to us as doing so.

But what, then, is freedom? As we noted, freedom is the possibility of variation, perhaps an infinite variation. This is at least the possibility that Tolstoy's analysis of the object seems expressly to permit. This is, perhaps, somewhat of an overstatement. As in Kant, freedom has a specific contour; it is a kind of self-legislation. But the difference between Tolstoyan self-legislation and that of Kant is considerable, for Tolstoy seems to allow a great deal more flexibility as to how reason might in fact define itself than Kant does, at least on the surface. And this is where the question about the nature of reason becomes so very complicated.

Fundamentally at issue is a comprehensive problem that one commentator has called the Kantian paradox.[12] This paradox might be expressed in simple fashion as describing the tension inherent in providing a definition of reason as an agency free to define itself, i.e. spontaneous. If reason is free to define itself, it is thus somewhat of an encroachment on that freedom to define reason as having to assume a specific identity. This is a tension appearing very distinctly in Tolstoy as well because infinite variation expressly provides for it; indeed, infinite variation is a way of defining spontaneity.

The upshot is that reason might be an agency with a particular role but no general identity in regard to how that role should be fulfilled: it is sovereign, yes, but the sovereign is elusive, as elusive as the god it replaces.

IV.

The most elusive concept in Tolstoy's treatise is thus freedom as the realm of "rational consciousness." Tolstoy strains to identify the kind of emancipation he sees as essential for a proper conception of life, an emancipation of course from the fetters of the "animal personality." But he is far less clear about what that emancipation might entail. In this respect, one fears a simple return to the hollow definition of freedom as "freedom from," a definition that is merely negative.

This fear is never fully averted since so much of the central portion of *On Life* consists of a dense, repetitive web of argument in which bare assertion prevails over explanation. One of the first of these assertions sets the tone for the rest:

Human life begins only with the appearance of a rational consciousness—the very thing that reveals to man his life in the present and in the past and the life of other entities, and all the suffering and death that inevitably results from the relations of these entities— the very thing that produces in him the negation of the good of the personal life and the contradiction, which, as it seems to him, arrests his life. (*OLMT,* 39)

[Жизнь человеческая начинается только с проявления разумного сознания,—того самого, которое открывает человеку одновременно и свою жизнь, и в настоящем и в прошедшем, и жизнь других личностей, и все, неизбежно вытекающее из отношений этих личностей, страдания и смерть,— то самое, что производит в нем отрицание блага личной жизни и противоречие, которое, ему кажется, останавливает его жизнь.] (*PSS* 26:342)

Rational consciousness discovers time and death. Rational consciousness ushers in an awareness not dissimilar from that which Rousseau associates with the birth of society: in both cases the innocence of animal immediacy is lost (Rousseau, 89). While the gift of reason for Rousseau is certainly not an unmixed blessing, for Tolstoy it takes on a much more positive quality. And it does so mainly because rational consciousness overcomes the borders established by time and space; as Tolstoy suggests, it is quite literally beyond time and space. This is indeed the precondition of its being able to think entities in time and space. To imagine entities inside time in space is of course to assume some exteriority, though the latter may be impossible of definition. Tolstoy is clear on this latter point for he says that "[r]eason cannot be defined" (*OLMT,* 47/*PSS* 26:347); yet, he also admits that "we have no need to define it, for not only do we all know it but it is the one thing we do know" (*OLMT,* 47/*PSS* 26:347).

Tolstoy fails to explain what kind of knowledge this might be. Once again, he multiplies formulations rather than explaining them.

He says that "[r]eason is what we know most surely and first of all"; that "it is impossible not to know it, for reason is the law by which rational beings—men—must live"; that reason "for man is the law by which his life is accomplished, just such a law as that for the animal by which it feeds itself and multiplies," a rather ironic statement given the crucial distinction between humans and animals that Tolstoy seems to seek to promote (*OLMT,* 47/*PSS* 26:348). Here is a peculiar vision of the *animal rationale* run amok. To be human is to be rational and to cleave to the law of reason that gives us a security surprisingly akin to animal instinct. That is all well and good, but one wonders why Tolstoy is so hesitant to give a more expansive account of what the law of reason is.

The closest Tolstoy comes to this kind of account is when he associates reason with unity and solidarity with other rational beings. To employ an allusive spatial metaphor, reason occupies for Tolstoy a unified realm in which all human beings can become one, leaving behind the artificial, if not defective quality of their being—their individuality. Tolstoy puts this rather bluntly, and his point is a remarkable one since he taps into a Platonic line of reasoning that emerges also in Kant.

The basic premise of this line of reasoning is that universality, a kind of unity, is the highest goal of human being. If we are rational beings, we tend to come together as one in reason which is one and the same for all. Particularity must be overcome, and only by overcoming particularity is one capable of becoming truly human. That is, particularity must consist of something that reason cannot adequately grasp. Instead of attributing failure to reason, the suggestion here is that the particular is a kind of failure since it resists unification or orderly classification.

Kant's position is formidably complex on this issue. But, from the point of view of practical philosophy, it is quite clear that Kant—at least for some time—held a similar view: to act morally is to act "universally" in accordance with duty (which, by definition, is universal). Kant's famous moral rigorism consists of his adamant refusal to refer to actions motivated by anything other than duty alone as truly moral: to be a moral being is to be a being that acts on universal principles. Thus, action that arises from particular motivations dependent on particular contexts should not be moral.

What really brings Tolstoy and Kant together here in regard to the identity of reason is the insistence on the universal, on the universalizing quality of reason as a defense against the particular. In Kantian terms, Tolstoy values the spontaneity of reason above the receptivity of the senses, this being another way of saying that Tolstoy values sapience over mere sentience, the ability to subordinate stimuli to a plan established from an agency utterly distinct from them as opposed to merely reacting willy-nilly in the nets of time.

V.

The primary Tolstoyan distinction in the treatise between animal personality and rational consciousness has thus a very Kantian flavor in so far as Tolstoy upholds, albeit in a far less technical way, the Kantian distinction between the empirical, the heteronymous, and the transcendental, the autonomous, aspects of the subject, one a seemingly passive vehicle of sense impressions, the other a locus of normative conceptual activity. Put in other terms, for Kant the empirical and transcendental are in fact aspects of the same subject, and it is one of the primary tasks of the Kantian enterprise to develop a consistent account of how these two aspects relate to each other. While Tolstoy affirms the two-aspect way of approaching subjecthood, he is rather more indirect about the relation between the two, though here, as elsewhere, he ultimately follows Kantian precedent.

What do I mean by this? It should first of all be astonishing to anyone that there could be such a relation. That is so because this relation is none other than that vexed relation of the particular and the general which I just mentioned and which plays such a large role in Tolstoy's treatise as a whole. For the animal personality seems to be the vehicle of the sense impression, the particular, while rational consciousness tends in the opposite direction entirely. Unlike Kant, Tolstoy seems to be far less optimistic about finding a ground of contact between these two realms: rather, they seem opposed. The reason for this lies securely in the infinite, what I have called, in relation to rational consciousness, infinite variability or, more succinctly, spontaneity. And, while Kant also ties reason to spontaneity, he hedges his bets.

The reason for Kant's hesitation is that spontaneity, as I have noted, would seem to suggest that there is no real law to reason, that reason is infinitely self-fashioning, and, indeed, if the understanding is the spontaneous creation of reason, one need not go far to conclude that the world caught in the nets of those concepts is a child of reason. If this is a rather daring interpretation of Kant that edges reason towards some notion of intellectual intuition, I am not sure that is the case with Tolstoy, at least not the Tolstoy of *On Life* who seems clearly to assimilate rational consciousness to intellectual intuition, pure spontaneity, even emptiness, to borrow an eastern notion of spontaneity that may fit Tolstoy quite nicely.[13] Hence, the attempts repeatedly made to meld the abstract discourse of philosophy with an ostensibly ordinary discourse about objects, one that tends to be more literary, are ways of bringing together two heterogeneous kinds of intuitive discourse: that of rational consciousness and that of the animal personality.

And this is where one finds some of the most interesting features of Tolstoy's treatise, its attempt to bring together these various kinds of discourse through the mediation of philosophy. Specifically, the treatise highlights a common feature of Tolstoy's ostensibly abstract writings: that they so often feature elaborate similes and models of thought drawn from relatively humble contexts, like that involving the miller, or, as we will see below, one involving a mule. The Tolstoyan move to metaphor and simile is a nod to the power of the empirical animal self, and a desire not simply to put this self aside. In a rather quiet way, Tolstoy chooses literary diversion over obliteration of the self.

Likewise Tolstoy develops his thinking in the context of another discourse, that of Christian thought. There is in fact a strong impetus in the treatise to reconcile the rationalist analysis with basic Christian tenets. Hence, the imputation of unity to rational consciousness and its expression of law become wholly compatible with Christian notions of unity and law. What is peculiar here, however, is that God, the essential basis for unity and law is not mentioned in Tolstoy's treatise at all; nor, for that matter, does Tolstoy speak of the soul or other of the supernatural entities that are the bedrock of faith.

But I should like to claim that, notwithstanding these elements of dissent, Tolstoy's treatise is attempting to create a new, presumably more holistic kind of writing that bridges the gap between philosophy, religion, and art as a way of modeling the integration between animal personality and rational consciousness, a relation of subordination to be sure, but still one in which a plurality of discourses may be refined and brought together.

The attempt to integrate discourses also provides a useful standpoint from which to consider the epigraphs to the treatise. Pascal's famous distinction between the *esprit de finesse* and the *esprit de géométrie* offers a guideline here (Pascal, 151–152). Pascal and Kant are antipodes in this regard, but it is of considerable interest that the epigraphs do not focus on their difference but their similarity. Both epigraphs rely on metaphors, and it could hardly be said that they show off their respective authors at their most abstract. Indeed, Tolstoy chooses what amount to a series of clichés, and of course this choice sheds light on the rhetorical concerns Tolstoy may have had with the treatise. Cliché in this respect is not to be understood as a term of opprobrium, though that association cannot admittedly be lightly pushed aside. To the contrary, cliché is the epitome of the successful general statement or understanding.

Yet, I think that even this rhetorical element, a way of seducing readers to what is more abstract, is merely the consequence of the broader attempt to integrate different kinds of discourse in a multivalent whole.[14] Whether this attempt succeeds or not should be a guiding concern as should its value to a proper understanding of the matters at hand: one cannot expect issues which occupied someone like Kant over three intricate critiques to be dealt with effectively in a relatively short treatise.

VI.

In a way typical of this aspect of the treatise, Tolstoy summarizes the freedom of reason through an extended simile:

> Renunciation (отречение) of the well-being (благо) of animal personality is the law of human life. If it is not accomplished freely, expressing itself in submission to reasonable consciousness, it is accomplished forcibly in each man at the bodily death of his animal personality, when under the weight of his sufferings he desires only one thing: to be released from the painful consciousness of his perishing personality and pass over to another kind (вид) of existence.
>
> The entry into life and the life of humankind are like what takes place when its master leads a horse out of the stable and puts it under harness. On coming out of the stable the horse, seeing the light of day and scenting liberty, imagines this liberty is life; but it is under harness and the reins are pulled. It feels a weight behind it, and if it thinks that its life consists in running about free it begins to struggle, falls, sometimes kills itself. If it does not kill itself, only two courses are open to it: either it draws its load and finds that it is not too heavy and that drawing it is not a misery but a joy, or else it becomes unmanageable and then the master takes it to a treadmill and ties it to the wall; the wheel turns under its feet and it goes round on one spot in the dark and suffers, but its strength is not expended in vain, it performs its involuntary task and the law is fulfilled—the difference is only that in the first case it works cheerfully, but in the second unwillingly and in misery. (*OLMT,* 70-71)

[Отречение от блага животной личности есть закон жизни человеческой. Если он не совершается свободно, выражаясь в подчинении разумному сознанию, то он совершается в каждом человеке насильно при плотской смерти его животного, когда он от тяжести страданий желает одного: избавиться от мучительного сознания погибающей личности и перейти в другой вид существования.

Вступление в жизнь и жизнь человека подобна тому, что совершается с лошадью, которую хозяин выводит из конюшни и впрягает. Лошади, выходящей из конюшни и увидавшей свет и почуявшей свободу, кажется, что в этой-то свободе и жизнь, но ее впрягают и трогают. Она чует за собой тяжесть и, если она думает, что жизнь ее в том, чтобы бегать на свободе, она начинает биться, падает, убивается иногда. Но если она не убьется, ей только два выхода: или она пойдет и повезет, и увидит, что тяжесть не велика и езда не мука, а радость, или отобьется от рук, и тогда хозяин сведет ее на рушильное колесо, привяжет арканом к стене, колесо завертится под ней, и она будет ходить в темноте на одном месте, страдая, но ее силы не пропадут даром: она сделает свою невольную работу, и закон исполнится и на ней. Разница будет только в том, что первая будет работать радостно, а вторая невольно и мучительно.] (*PSS* 26:366)

This passage brings us back to the beginning of my essay. Here Tolstoy provides his own summary of his argument. Notably, it centers on a homey simile. In doing so, it seems that Tolstoy makes an attempt to bring together the various kinds of discourse. But why does he does so? There is, after all, more than a little irony in using a homey image to describe a kind of existence that has nothing to do with that image.

In this sense, the treatise is corrupt, or seems to be so. And, perhaps, Tolstoy is arguing that the corruption cannot be eradicated, that the treatise itself must have recourse to a language which it would work to undermine; the problem being, in this latter case, that no language can adequately describe rational consciousness as it is: to reify it would be to lose it. In other words, Tolstoy's assimilation of rational conscious-ness to a kind of intuition, and intellectual intuition, tends to subtract it from the realm of discourse, since discourse always works in time and has to be scanned successively. For intuition, there is only immediacy, for discourse, mediacy. This basic tension passes through the entire trea-tise and sheds light on the curious competition, perhaps, between dif-ferent kinds of discourse in it. The multiplicity of the means exploited in the treatise to describe the relation between animal consciousness and rational consciousness is the mirror of their problematic interre-lation.

One might argue more ambitiously that this crucial interrelation, bequeathed to us, by a complex tradition, is at the heart of Tolstoy's ever shifting alliances, and, thus, of his attempts in so many different forms of discourse to find the proper language of rational conscious-ness, the proper language of the gods which we have forgotten or are too hard of hearing to hear.

(Notes)

1   In this essay, I employ the term "rational" instead of "reasonable" to translate the adjective "разумный" in the expression "разумное сознание" or "rational consciousness." I do so because, in my view, "reasonable" does not adequately describe the range of meaning, speculative and practical, that the term seems to have in Tolstoy's treatise. In English "reasonable" has a strongly and simplistically pragmatic orientation that does not include the kind of speculative reasoning of which "rational consciousness" is capable. Indeed, the echo of Kantian *Vernunft* is not captured well by "reasonable"—one speaks of theoretical and practical *rationality* in Kant (and elsewhere) and not of theoretical and practical *reasonableness*. And one does so despite the fact that the relevant German adjective, *vernünftig*, can be an equivalent for "reasonable" in conventional speech.

2   I might note that Kant explicitly refers to Leibniz more than any other philosopher, both in the critical and the pre-critical periods: one should not forget the importance of the Leibniz-Wolff school in shaping Kant's philosophical orientation. See Jauernig, 41.

3   See, for example, Heidegger, 7–29. Heidegger maintains that only poetry is of the same rank as philosophy, the dogmatism inherent in Christianity being for him a sign of the latter's weakness in relation both to philosophy and poetry.

4   Clowes makes a somewhat similar claim for the originality of Russian philosophy (Clowes, 1-14).

5   Tolstoy's contemporaries were inclined to identify a much more direct influence. On this issue, and as an astute consideration of Tolstoy's relation to philosophers, please see Scanlan.

6   To be sure, one can object that this concern, whose classical articulation belongs to David Hume, pertains to modern, Post-Cartesian thought as a whole and is thus hardly the property of Kant alone. While the objection is a justifiable one, I suspect that the relation of facts and values in its broader context, as a questioning of the scientific understanding of life, becomes fully articulate more sharply in Rousseau than in Hume and, then, with unsurpassed rigor and complexity, in Kant, particularly as interpreted by the two primary Neo-Kantian schools.

7   For an interesting argument against this view, see Crary.

8   Weber cites Tolstoy's critique of science with approval in his important talk, "Science as a Vocation." See Weber, 17–18.

9   All references to the text of *On Life* refer first to the pagination of the translation by Aylmer and Louise Maude (see Tolstoy) and then to the Russian edition published in volume 26 of *PSS*.

10   The importance of the infinite to *War and Peace* is marked by discussions in the so-called essays. *A Confession* also refers frequently to the infinite.

11   See Deleuze, 39–72.

12   See Pippin, 45.

13   Tolstoy's interest in Buddhism and Taoism is well known. In the latter case,

Denner gives an interesting account of Tolstoy's encounter with the notion of wu-wei, non-action or action without intent.

14   Note Nietzsche's famous aphorism in *Beyond Good and Evil*: "The more abstract the truth you wish to teach us, the more you must entice our senses into learning it" (Nietzsche, 66). No truth could be more abstract than infinite variability, hence, the necessity for figuration. But, one wonders what can be learned from figuration.

Works Cited:

Badiou, Alain. *Being and Event*. Tr. Oliver Feltham. London: Continuum, 2005

Brandom, Robert. *Making It Explicit: Reasoning, Representing and Discursive Commitment*. Cambridge, MA: Harvard UP, 1994

Clowes, Edith. *Fiction's Overcoat: Russian Literary Culture and the Question of Philosophy*. Ithaca, NY: Cornell UP, 2004

Crary, Alice. *Beyond Moral Judgment*. Cambridge, MA: Harvard UP, 2009

Deleuze, Gilles. *Nietzsche & Philosophy*. Tr. Hugh Tomlinson. New York: Columbia UP, 1983

Denner, Michael. "Tolstoyan Nonaction: The Advantage of Doing Nothing." *Tolstoy Studies Journal* 13 (2001): 8–22

Heidegger, Martin. *Introduction to Metaphysics*. Tr. Gregory Fried and Richard Polt. New Haven: Yale UP, 1999

Jauernig, Anja. "Kant's Critique of the Leibnizian Philosophy: *Contra* the Leibnizians but *Pro* Leibniz." *Kant and the Early Moderns*. Ed. Daniel Garber and Béatrice Longuenesse. Princeton: Princeton UP, 2008

Nietzsche, Friedrich. *Beyond Good and Evil*. Tr. Marion Faber. Oxford: Oxford World's Classics, 1998

Pascal, Blaise. *Pensées*. Tr. Honor Levi. Oxford: Oxford World's Classics, 1995

Pippin, Robert. *Modernism as a Philosophical Problem*. 2nd ed. Oxford: Blackwell, 1999

Rousseau, Jean-Jacques. *Discourse on the Origins and Foundations of Inequality among Men*. Tr. Maurice Cranston. London: Penguin, 1984

Scanlan, James. "Tolstoy among the Philosophers: His Book *On Life* and Its Critical Reception." *Tolstoy Studies Journal* 15 (2006): 52–69

(*OLMT*) Tolstoy, Leo. *On Life and Essays on Religion*. Tr. Aylmer Maude. Oxford: Oxford UP, 1934

(*PSS*) Толстой, Л .Н. *Полное собрание сочинений в 90 томах, академическое юбилейное издание*. Москва: Государственное издательство художественной литературы, 1928–58

Weber, Max. *The Vocation Lectures: "Science as a Vocation," "Politics as a Vocation."* Tr. Rodney Livingstone. Indianapolis, IN: Hackett Publishing, 2004

Tolstoy's Implausible Theodicy: The Justification of Suffering in *On Life*

James Scanlan
Ohio State University

The discussion of suffering in the last two chapters of *On Life*, the most deliberately and exclusively philosophical of all Leo Tolstoy's works, poses a dilemma for anyone who seeks to judge the master story-teller and moralist as a philosopher. On the one hand, the discussion seems to rebut those critics past and present who have held that Tolstoy had no real understanding of what a philosophical problem is, for in these chapters he appears to comprehend and to address appropriately a thorny issue that has occupied theologians and philosophers for centuries.[1] On the other hand, even though he advances relevant, logically valid arguments in support of his position on the issue, the premises on which he bases his arguments are so far-fetched, and his avoidance of hard questions about his position is so glaring, that the dissatisfaction of the philosophical critics is quite understandable.

The issue in question is the hoary "problem of evil." Its paradigmatic statement was offered by the ancient Greek philosopher Epicurus and others, who used it to cast doubt on the idea that the natural world was created by a spiritual, personal God Who is both benevolent and omnipotent. The difficulty with such a view, according to the skeptics, is that the world is full of suffering and other forms of evil, the presence of which would seem to show that the Creator either does not care that people suffer (and so is not benevolent) or is powerless to prevent it (and so is not omnipotent). It was the need to account for the presence of such pervasive evils as suffering in a divinely created world—in Milton's apt phrase, to "justify the ways of God to men"—that have given rise to the various theodicies produced by Christian thinkers.

Although Tolstoy by no means advances a theistic conception of the world in *On Life*, the world view he does advance, claiming it to be thoroughly "rational," also requires the functional equivalent of a theodicy. By this time (1888) in his long spiritual quest he had largely rejected belief in a perfect and all-powerful creator in favor of a more pantheistic or panentheistic conception of reality as a spiritual whole that is fully comprehensible and intelligible to human reason.[2] In this way he avoided the problem of evil in its traditional form. But even without assuming a perfect creator, he is still obliged to justify the presence of negative phenomena such as death and suffering in a cosmic system that is supposedly perfect—perfect not because it was created by a supremely good and powerful deity, but because it incorporates a comprehensive rationality that should brook no such blights as the senseless suffering inflicted on the guiltless by natural disasters, epidemics, wars, and crime. Tolstoy never calls his reflections here a 'theodicy', but in his relentless drive to prove the rationality of his world view he is faced with the same task any theodicist faces—to justify the apparent evils of the world as he conceives it. If he did not recognize the philosophical need for this, why would he devote the concluding chapters of this work to suffering?

* * *

In the earlier chapters of *On Life*, Tolstoy had established to his own satisfaction that bodily death is not incompatible with the notion of a fully rational universe, so long as the truly spiritual and hence eternal nature of the self is admitted. But in the two concluding chapters he confronts the kinds of horrors that led Ivan Karamazov to return his "ticket" to the supposed "higher harmony" that some theodicists had imagined as the grand purpose justifying such regrettable but necessary evils as the sufferings of innocent children. In *The Brothers Karamazov*, Dostoevsky had presented through Ivan Karamazov a wrenching picture of child abuse, using terms quite compatible with Tolstoy's non-theistic approach—that is, as simply a question of the rationality or intelligibility of such phenomena. "I can understand nothing of why it's all arranged as it is," Ivan Karamazov cries; "it's quite incomprehensible why they [innocent children] should have to suffer, and why they should buy harmony with their suffering." Although Ivan's challenge carries great emotional force, it is essentially an intellectual challenge: "Can you understand such nonsense?" he asks Alyosha.[3] Tolstoy, without mentioning either Ivan or Dostoevsky himself, is in effect taking up Ivan's challenge in the final two chapters of *On Life*. He is seeking to establish that the presence of suffering in the world is understandable, that it does not contravene reason.

At the outset Tolstoy makes no effort to deny the importance of suffering; he even appears to call at least some of it inexplicable. In the opening sentence of Chapter 34 he acknowledges the existence of "terrible, pointless sufferings," unjustified sufferings that "can never be averted" and are enough to "destroy any rational meaning [разумный смысл] attributed to life" (*PSS* 26:423). Asking further what purpose such sufferings could possibly have, he affirms that "rational explanations [рассудочные объясения] explain nothing. They always avoid the very essence of the question and serve only to show its unanswerability more convincingly" (*PSS* 26:424). It will be noted, however, that in the course of a few lines Tolstoy has switched between two Russian adjectives for 'rational'—*разумный* and *рассудочный*—which are derived from two Russian words for 'reason,' разум and рассудок. The two words differ considerably in connotation, and the distinction between them, though unremarked by Tolstoy at this point, is central to the complex and curious case he proceeds to make for the reasonableness of suffering, as we shall see below. Here his comments simply leave open the possibility that even if suffering is irrational according to *рассудок*, it may be rational according to *разум*.

In the discussion that follows, Tolstoy proceeds to argue that suffering *is* in fact rational in the latter sense, and hence perfectly understandable. In making his case for the reasonableness of a world full of sufferings he draws on a complex of assumptions about human beings and their experiences that he appears to consider essentially obvious to a reasonable person and thus in no need of explicit support. In fact he does support them indirectly, however, by offering comments and examples that illustrate or suggest them in various ways. These premises, if true, would provide him with a solid logical foundation for his justification of suffering, but at least at first glance they appear to vary considerably in plausibility, ranging from those, on the one hand, that are unobjectionable even to critics of theodicies, to those, on the other hand, that strain credulity to the limit.

His first, uncontroversial, assumption is that suffering serving some more important purpose is reasonable and cannot be considered bad. Physical pain, for example, is in many cases a valuable protective mechanism for the animal organism—"the first and foremost means of both preserving our bodies and prolonging our animal life" (*PSS* 26:431), as when a burn teaches a child not to touch a hot stove. Tolstoy strengthens that claim to the point of calling pain "an indispensable condition of one's animal as well as rational life" (*PSS* 26:433). If childbirth were not painful, he argues, women would produce too many children to support, and if youthful excesses did not have painful consequences, "children and young people would thoroughly ruin their whole bodies" (*PSS* 26:433). Generalizing, he describes suffering very broadly as "a painful sensation that produces activity that eliminates the painful sensation and produces a state of pleasure" (*PSS* 26:425). His examples may not always be the most convincing, but few critics would deny that some suffering, at least, can be justified on the basis of its instrumental value. Only an anti-Leibnizian dreamer would insist that a world in which no pleasures required pains would be still more reasonable.

The second assumption is that suffering for moral misdeeds is justifiable. When it results from my own bad actions, Tolstoy argues, suffering "is what it ought to be," and as a result I "bear it lightly and often gladly" (*PSS* 26:428–29). Indeed, he continues, underlining the universality of suffering, "half the life of every person passes in sufferings that he not only does not regard as agonizing . . . but even considers good for him, simply because they are endured as the consequences of errors" (*PSS* 26:430). Disregarding some possible overstatement of the joys of suffering on Tolstoy's part here, we may agree with him that it is reasonable to believe that some people may deserve to be punished for misdeeds, especially given the fact that such punishment may in addition have instrumental value of the kind allowed by his first assumption, because it could serve as a motive for moral improvement by "directing his activity toward the elimination of the error" (*PSS* 26:428). But over and above its value as a moral corrective, Tolstoy also regards suffering as justifiable penance for doing wrong; both considerations figure in his defense of punishment for misdeeds, and here again many moralists would agree with him.

The first two assumptions provide justifications of instrumental suffering and of suffering as morally deserved punishment, but to most critics of theodicy these types of suffering are not the problem. The problem is suffering that seems pointless and undeserved—the suffering of an innocent victim of a crime, an earthquake victim, a casualty of war, disease, or famine. Tolstoy himself grants that there appears to be a "great mass of suffering" in human life for which the individual bears no personal responsibility and which serves no reasonable purpose— cases, he writes, in which "a person is afflicted by suffering that goes beyond any visible connection between suffering and wrongdoing, such as when he suffers from causes that have always been outside his own activity, or when the consequences of his suffering can be of no use either to himself or to anyone else" (*PSS* 26:428). These are the sufferings that most demand explanation in a supposedly reasonable world.

Tolstoy takes a major step into this murky territory with a third assumption, never explicitly stated but central to his reasoning here— namely, that strictly speaking there are no fully "innocent victims," for all men are sinners and in that respect are producers of suffering themselves. This principle of universal guilt is implicit throughout Chapter 34 of *On Life*. Only the self-deluded individual, Tolstoy writes, fails to recognize "those sins of his by which he has brought suffering into the world" (*PSS* 26:430). There is no reference to the theological doctrine of original sin here, but Tolstoy takes for granted that sinfulness, like suffering itself, is an inescapable part of the human condition; in regard to sinfulness, human beings differ in degree only. "The whole of a person's life from the first days of childhood," he states, "consists in this alone: in becoming aware of sin through suffering and freeing the oneself from errors" (*PSS* 26:430).

Tolstoy's principle of universal guilt sets the stage, finally, for the sweeping defense of suffering that he produces in these chapters of *On Life*, for it gives him a universal feature of the human condition that he can connect with the universal fact of suffering. His quite explicit statement of this connection takes the form of a fourth assumption on which his justification of suffering is based, and it is his most controversial assumption. From one point of view, it is a logical tour de force, but from another it is a wildly implausible generalization about human life that, far from being "rational," is difficult to take seriously. This generalization, to which he brooks no exceptions, is that *all* suffering is caused by sin. "My sins," Tolstoy writes, "whatever they may be, are the cause of my sufferings, whatever they may be" (*PSS* 26:429). Sin is not only a cause of suffering common to all humanity, it is the *only* cause of suffering. There is no suffering that cannot be traced to moral wrongdoing.

I call this assumption a logical tour de force because at a stroke it allows the admitted justifications of the reasonableness of suffering in some cases—where it is deserved because of moral culpability and where it has instrumental value—to apply to *all* cases of suffering without exception. First, *all* suffering is deserved, because all men are morally culpable; all deserve punishment for their misdeeds. Second, *all* suffering has instrumental value, because all suffering serves to remind people of their sinful ways and motivates them, as the children's burn does, to change those ways. Disregarding the seeming implausibility of this fourth assumption, from a strictly logical standpoint Tolstoy's premises taken together do provide a logical explanation for the existence of suffering, for they make all suffering a deserved response to the immoral actions of human beings and also invest it with the instrumental value of serving to prompt people to change their immoral behavior.

It may be logical, but is it a good explanation? A good explanation requires not only a valid logical structure but true premises to ground that structure, and the status of Tolstoy's fourth premise in particular—that all suffering is caused by sin—is clearly questionable. What, if anything, supports its claim to truth? Tolstoy's only argument for it is simply the equally dubious assertion that it is universally acknowledged to be true: "Man always recognizes suffering of every sort," he writes, "as the consequence of his sin" (*PSS* 26:430). One is tempted to read this as an echo of the age-old religious folk conviction that suffering is divine punishment for sin—one's own sins and/or the collective sins of the community. Tolstoy, however, does not phrase it in religious terms; he presents the premise not as an expression of faith but as something that a rational being knows immediately and directly—a product, in other words, of what philosophers call 'rational intuition', though he does not use that term. As such it requires not argumentative support but simply the "acknowledgment," as he frequently asserts, of an evident truth. Reason in effect speaks to me, and I "realize" that all suffering is caused by sin; this realization is a function of "the rational [разумное] consciousness" (*PSS* 26:427). Here Tolstoy is explicitly subscribes to the venerable philosophical theory of innate knowledge: "I know," he writes, "that I came into this life with a certain knowledge of the truth" (*PSS* 26:430), apparently including the "law of reason" that all suffering is caused by sin.

Surely, however, for this law to be known by reason, we must be able also to recognize a causal connection between sin and suffering in particular cases. For rational persons to accept that their suffering is deserved, and therefore serves to remind them of the need to repent and mend their ways, they must be able to trace it plausibly to some sin on their part. But in a great many cases of suffering in the real world it is by no means clear that a causal link to sin can be established or even imagined. For example, when I am the victim of a vicious, unprovoked attack by another person, what is the causal link that makes *me* deserve the punishment that is being inflicted on me? Again, turning to suffering from natural causes, what is the causal connection between any sin of mine and my death in an earthquake? Finally, how can the suffering of Ivan Karamazov's pitiful little child—or any child—be tied to sinfulness on the child's part?

The critical point at issue is the problem of identifying particular causal connections that allow us to justify the suffering that supposedly results from the sufferer's sin. Tolstoy clearly recognizes this, for in the final two chapters of *On Life* he plunges headlong into the metaphysical thickets of causality, community, and the cosmos in a vigorous attempt to cope with the problem. Although his arguments here leave much unstated and unclarified, his central points are clear enough, and they provide us with a richer view of his metaphysics and epistemology at this point in his life.

The first indication of his approach to the problem is found in his discussion of a hypothetical situation. A hunter is being attacked by a pack of wolves in the forest. The hunter, Tolstoy acknowledges, will understandably be preoccupied by thoughts of how to free himself from the wolves. But, Tolstoy goes on, the hunter as a "rational being" should also be thinking about something else: he should be remembering that in the past he has killed and eaten great numbers of animals, and he should recognize that sinful past behavior as the cause of his present suffering in the forest. In that light, Tolstoy maintains, the rational thing for the hunter to do in his predicament is to "acknowledge the sin that has produced the suffering, repent of it, and confess the truth" (*PSS* 26:426).

It is tempting to think that Tolstoy, in asking us to view past sin as the "cause" of present suffering in the case of the hunter, is simply appealing to a sense of poetic justice: the hunter is only "getting what he deserved" by being punished for his past transgressions—indeed, punished in the same violent way by creatures of the same kind he has violated in the past. If that were an adequate interpretation, Tolstoy would mean no more by "causation" here than a relation of moral appropriateness between sin and suffering. But poetic justice is more at home in literature than in philosophy, and Tolstoy in his role as philosopher appears to have a stronger, more direct and substantive causal connection in mind—as indeed he must have, if he wishes to find a causal connection in the multitude of cases in which no poetic justice is evident, such as suffering from purely natural causes and the suffering of small children.

In the case of the hunter and every other instance of suffering, Tolstoy proceeds to argue, although there may be no empirically evident causal connection between the suffering and the sufferer's sin, there is in fact such a connection that every rational person can discern. The "reason" that provides this knowledge is just the разум that he distinguishes from the lower, "animal" form of reason for which he uses the term рассудок, and it is here that the distinction becomes critical to his argument. Reasoning based on рассудок, he maintains, understands only the "external meaning of life"—only those connections between conduct and suffering that are visible to the person as an individual. The higher, truly human reason—разум—understands the "internal meaning" of the connection between suffering and sin because it does not confine the good to "the good of my separate personal life." Rather, it perceives the organic, spiritual union of all individuals and "recognizes as the good the good of my entire past and future life in an uninterrupted union with the good of other people and beings" (*PSS* 26:429). Thus the "internal connection of cause and action, which is always known to man from his rational [разумный] consciousness," links the sufferings of each with the guilt of all. No one should be "indignant at the sufferings he endures for the sins of the world," for his *own* sins are an integral part of that cosmic mass of evil (*PSS* 26:430).

In seeking the sources of suffering, Tolstoy contends, only the person whose life is confined to promoting the animal interests of his own individual well-being limits himself to material, spatiotemporal links of cause and effect, "phenomena that are visible to him" (*PSS* 26:429). I recognize that I suffer from hunger, for example, because I did not work to provide myself with food. This is a conclusion of рассудок. The man of разум, on the other hand, who is aware of the place of his immaterial, timeless self in the universal cosmic community, recognizes the invisible connections that tie individuals' actions and experiences to each other and to the community in a way that is not explicable in empirical terms but is nonetheless intelligible to, and indeed demanded by, the rational (разумный) consciousness. The external, visible bonds of cause and effect, such as my actions as a hunter and the suffering of the animals I kill, are not the same as "the internal connection of cause and action" always known to the rational consciousness, such as the link between my acts of killing in the past and my suffering as a victim of the wolves in the present.

The organic, spiritual union of individuals (and their actions) with "the good of other people and beings," which Tolstoy asks us to accept on the basis of our "rational consciousness," is described no further in this text. As he presents it here, it is hardly distinguishable from the classic "One" of mystical consciousness—that is, a transempirical unity that cannot be described in spatiotemporal terms, cannot be explained conceptually, but engulfs all its elements so that each affects the other. At this extreme of разум, rationality for Tolstoy merges into mysticism and defies discursive definition. From another standpoint, it also merges into ethics, for blindness to the spiritual union is attributed to selfish concentration on one's own person.

The minimum of explanation that Tolstoy does provide of the unseen causal bonds that exist in the spiritual union of individuals is couched mostly in terms of the relations among mature human beings, all of whom are assumed to be sinners. However difficult it may be, outside of a mystical transport, to accept as fully reasonable a world in which, for example, individuals not only suffer but *deserve* to suffer because of the sins of others, Tolstoy's story of unseen bonds provides an explanation that is at least relevant, if not convincing. By limiting the account to suffering produced by the evil actions of human beings, the story makes all the suffering that I as a sinner endure, even if seemingly remote from my own sinfulness, actually a product of the latter because of my complicity in creating the organic mass of evil in the community.

But does that story really show that *all* suffering is caused by the sinfulness of the victim, as Tolstoy insists? For two remaining classes of suffering, the answer would seem to be No. These are, first, suffering that seems to have no human agency as its immediate cause, and hence cannot be attributed to anyone's sinfulness, whether the sufferers' themselves or that of others; and, second, the suffering of young children, who cannot be considered sinners themselves and seem undeserving of suffering from the sinfulness of others. These are the two great classes of suffering on which many theodicies have foundered, and up to this point in our examination of Tolstoy's analysis of suffering we have not yet seen a direct explanation of either.

Surprisingly, the first class—suffering the immediate cause of which is non-human agency, such as natural disasters—Tolstoy largely ignores in these chapters. He certainly acknowledges its existence, and he emphasizes the difficulty of explaining it; it is, of course, completely inexplicable from the standpoint of рассудок, which understands only empirical, "external" relations of cause and effect. But once he has sketched the mystical metaphysics that validates "internal," unseen bonds of cause and effect and declared in no uncertain terms that *all* suffering is caused by the sinfulness of the victim, he never returns to explain how this "law" could possibly apply to the suffering produced, most directly and visibly, by earthquakes, famines, and other natural causes. He does note one explanation sometimes offered—namely, that such suffering is necessary in order to teach people lessons, such as the need to erect sturdier buildings, be more careful with fire, and avoid contracting social diseases. But he scornfully dismisses that suggestion because, he says, it leaves out "an enormous class of sufferings that it cannot explain" (*PSS* 26:429). Yet he himself does not discuss how the attribution of all suffering to sin explains the still more enormous class of *all* suffering produced by natural causes.

Tolstoy does, however, provide one hint of a direction such an explanation might take, had he been inclined to follow it—namely, expansion of his "spiritual community" to include nonhuman entities. The hint comes in the very passage in which he develops the idea of "unseen bonds." The hypothetical hunter, it will be remembered, is being attacked not by other human beings but by wolves, and yet the hunter's own past sinfulness, Tolstoy holds, is the ultimate cause of his suffering. The causal chain that leads back from the immediate cause of suffering to the victim's sins, Tolstoy must be assuming, includes bonds between human and non-human causes. Noteworthy in the same passage, too, is the fact that in characterizing the spiritual community within which the "unseen bonds" exist, Tolstoy describes it as a community of "people and beings" (люди и существа), not simply people. Clearly he does not limit it to human beings and their actions, for the suffering in his hypothetical case is inflicted by wolves.

But if wolves can be included in the causal chain, why not earthquakes and floods, so that natural disasters, too, could be somehow connected through unseen bonds with the sinfulness of the victim? Of this possibility, however, there is not even a hint in these chapters. The Russian term for "beings" (существа) that Tolstoy employs in describing the spiritual community typically refers to animate beings only, and there is no indication that Tolstoy meant to include *inanimate* things in his moral universe. Yet this is just what he would need to do in order to bring suffering from natural disasters within explanatory range, given his other assumptions and premises. His spiritual community of "people and beings" would have to include not only animals but rivers, fires, and tectonic plates, and he would have to attribute to them a moral identity that provides them with the capacity to sin, such that they, too would be integrated into the cosmic interplay of sin and suffering that he describes.[4] Insisting that all suffering is caused by sin, he failed to provide any plausible explanation of suffering the immediate cause of which is non-human.

By contrast with his reticence in that area, Tolstoy goes on in the brief final chapter of *On Life* to confront directly the second questionable class of sufferings—those of innocent children. Although children, as human beings, would seem indisputably to be members of Tolstoy's spiritual community of "people and beings," apparently he was not comfortable with ascribing to them the same sinfulness that characterizes its full members and produces its suffering. Consequently he appears to exempt them from the principle of universal guilt. But if they are not sinful, why do they suffer?

Confronted with this theoretical question, Tolstoy confidently offers a quite unexpected answer, one that would surely astonish Ivan Karamazov. In what may be the weakest argument in the long history of theodicies, he attempts to show that the experiences we call "suffering" in children are not really suffering at all, or at least not suffering to any significant degree.

However startling this approach may be, it is a perfectly logical line of argument for Tolstoy, given his insistence that all suffering is caused by the sinfulness of the sufferer. Faced with the apparent counterexample of suffering, innocent children he could, on the one hand, have tried to show that the children are not really innocent, whether by reason of being marked by original sin, or being at least *potential* sinners, or being organic parts of the sinful community of "people and beings" and hence sharing mystically in its guilt. But, on the other hand, it is equally logical to take a different tack and try to question, as he does, not the children's innocence but their suffering. There is no need to be disturbed by the suffering of children if in fact they do not suffer, or suffer only to a negligible extent.

Tolstoy begins the chapter by shifting suddenly from the unqualified term "suffering" (страдание) to the expressions "bodily suffering" (телесное страдание) or, more frequently, simply "pain" (боль). This shift is central to what he wishes to argue, which is that, strictly speaking, only mature human beings suffer, whereas what is felt by the lower animals and immature human beings such as children, in whom "rational [разумное] consciousness has not yet awakened" (*PSS* 26:432), is merely bodily discomfort or pain, a far less distressing experience. "Pain in the animal and in the child," he writes, "is very limited and small in magnitude, never reaching the agony it reaches in a being endowed with rational consciousness" (*PSS* 26:431).

To those who might object to this last contention, Tolstoy offers (with all the authority of the paterfamilias of Yasnaya Polyana) two purportedly factual claims about children's pain. The first is that a child's outward expression of pain is "immeasurably greater than the suffering itself" and misleads us into feeling more sympathy for the little one than is rationally appropriate. The child, he declares, "sometimes cries as piteously from a fleabite as from a pain that destroys its internal organs." The cries are heart-rending, but the pain "is more our suffering than theirs" (*PSS* 26:431). His second reason for considering the pain of children insignificant is that it is, he contends, never intense enough even to be remembered by the child: "The pain of an unreasoning being leaves no traces in the memory," he writes, adding that in later life people cannot even imagine, much less remember, the so-called "sufferings" of their childhood (*PSS* 26:431). Tolstoy alludes to other differences between pain and suffering as well, but they do not alter his essential point—that, strictly speaking, children do not suffer: "In essence, only when we are in full possession of our rational consciousness can we even speak of sufferings, because it is only with this condition that life and those states of it that we call sufferings even begin" (*PSS* 26:432).

Why do we need "rational consciousness" in order to suffer? Because, as Tolstoy appears to be arguing at the very end of his final chapter, truly human suffering requires an intellectual act of recognition—the recognition of an unmet moral obligation to rid the world of sin, whether one's own or that of others. Here are his words:

> There is but one suffering for man . . . . That suffering is the consciousness of the contradiction between the sinfulness of oneself and the whole world and not merely the opportunity but the obligation, not simply for someone but for me myself, to turn the full truth into a reality not only in my own life but in that of the entire world. (*PSS* 26:434)

Only a mature human being—someone, as he says, "in full possession" of a rational consciousness (*PSS* 26:432)—knows that there is a "contradiction" between the sinful world as it is and the world as it should be, knows the "full truth" about what it should be, and knows that it is his personal responsibility to work to implement that full truth. A young child cannot be aware of all this; consequently, a young child cannot suffer—not even, it seems, when its internal organs are being destroyed.

* * *

Tolstoy's surprising dismissal of the suffering of young children helps to make clear, I believe, why his attempt at a theodicy in these last two chapters is so unsatisfying. Although he writes throughout as though he were seeking a comprehensive explanation of human suffering, there is really only one type of suffering that truly interests him: it is the suffering of moral guilt, of being conscious of one's own sinfulness and of the obligation to correct it. Despite the fact that at times he characterizes suffering very broadly as "painful sensation" (болезненное ощущение) (*PSS* 26:425), his attention always gravitates toward the species of painful sensation that is moral guilt. For him it is the most severe of human sufferings, the type for which he typically reserves terms such as "agony" (мучительность) and "terrifying torment" (ужасающая мука) (*PSS* 26:431, 427). Indeed, as we saw above, at times he goes so far as to deny the very application of the term "suffering" to any other form of discomfort, as when he equates guilt caused by sinfulness with "the condition which we call suffering."

It would be clearer if he had written "which *I* call suffering," for in practice he simply resists the use of the term for any other situation, limiting it to a highly specific experience of human beings which he calls variously "true suffering," "human suffering," or, most confusingly, simply "suffering." His attitude toward all other sorts of pain or so-called "suffering" is dismissive. In the case of children, it is too insignificant to warrant attention; his focus on moral guilt is so intense that he cannot consider dealing with the discomforts of those who have no shred of it. In other cases, the suffering is not troublesome because it has redeeming instrumental value. As for purely physical pain, he contends it is easily handled by a right-thinking person; he devotes several sentences to arguing that it is completely manageable by a rational individual, in the sense that it can be "reduced to an infinitely small amount" by someone with the right attitude toward it. More than that, it is possible "to reduce it to insensibility, even to the feeling of joy in enduring it." (*PSS* 26:432)

This same disinterest in suffering other than the suffering of moral guilt may well account for Tolstoy's lack of attention to the suffering produced by natural causes. Such causes have no obvious moral dimension at all, and the "suffering" they produce consists primarily if not exclusively in "merely" physical pain.

Furthermore, the intense focus on the suffering of moral guilt is surely responsible for Tolstoy's sweeping claim that all suffering is caused by sin. Obviously the statement is true if we limit it to "real suffering" or "true suffering" in Tolstoy's understanding of those expressions, which *equates* suffering with the consciousness of one's own sinfulness. And since, in comparison with the "terrifying torment" of that experience, all other species of suffering are negligible, they and their possible causes readily drop out of the theodicist's consideration.

What this all means, of course, is that what Tolstoy has presented in these chapters is not a justification of suffering in general but a justification of what is for him the only suffering that really matters—the suffering of moral guilt. As a theodicy, then, his argument here might most simply be summarized as follows: Since the ultimate cause of true human suffering (meaning by that the tormenting consciousness of moral guilt) is the sinfulness of the sufferers themselves, all such suffering is in effect self-inflicted. The sufferers themselves, as free creatures, are responsible for it and by the same token can eliminate it, if they so choose, by repenting and actively seeking the good. When they choose sin, it is understandable that suffering exists because it is reasonable that people suffer for their misdeeds and because it serves a valuable purpose as a spur to correcting their behavior. Further, it is reason that allows us to understand the source of suffering and tells us how to assuage it. "Reason says," Tolstoy writes, "that a person who acknowledges the connection of his sins and his sufferings with the sins and sufferings of the world, frees himself from the agony of suffering" (*PSS* 26:430).

This is "reasonable" enough as far as it goes, but the problem is that explaining the reasonableness of the agony of moral guilt is not justifying human suffering in general. Moral guilt is but one variety of the torments of men. All other suffering, from that of the victims of the great Lisbon earthquake of 1755 to that of Ivan Karamazov's piteous child, is effectively excluded from the scope of Tolstoy's argument.

The last two chapters of *On Life* are less a justification of human suffering than an ethical homily on the pervasiveness of moral guilt and how to assuage it. They are a ringing moral exhortation, a proclamation of the doctrine of universal moral responsibility: everyone is personally responsible for correcting the evils of the world. Tolstoy's homily may have the appearance of grappling systematically with the problem of evil; but in the end, rather than justifying the existence of suffering in general, he eliminates most of it from serious consideration in favor of the suffering that he, for whatever reason, found most anguishing.

Tolstoy's philosophical failure in these chapters consists in neither a misunderstanding of the problem of evil nor an inability to defend a position logically. It cannot be denied that he recognized suffering as a challenge to his rational cosmos or that he strove mightily to enlist reason in support of his response to that challenge. His failure consists, rather, in having his attention enthralled by ethical interests that led him to regard moral evil as the only true evil in the world and moral guilt as the only true suffering, the only suffering worth the close attention of the theodicist.

(Notes)

1   In his entry on Tolstoy for the Macmillan *Encyclopedia of Philosophy*, for example, Eugene Kamenka wrote that "Tolstoy . . . had no genuine conception of a philosophical problem or of a technical philosophical argument" (Kamenka, 147).

2   Although many commentators have characterized Tolstoy's mature world view as "pantheism", Richard Gustafson argues persuasively that it is more appropriately called "panentheism," since Tolstoy held that God is not only immanent in the world but also transcendent to it (but *not* as a creator). See Gustafson, 100–02.

3   Dostoevsky, 242–44.

4   Ironically, such an integration is not unknown in subsequent Russian philosophy. The twentieth-century panpsychist Nikolai Lossky (1870–1965), inspired by Leibniz's monadology, developed an elaborate metaphysical system that gives freedom of choice and the capacity to sin to every entity in the world, right down to subatomic particles, which he regards as proto-persons. In this respect, Tolstoy, lacking a metaphysics as rich as Lossky's, left his theodicy in *On Life* incomplete.

Works Cited:

Dostoevsky, Fyodor. *The Brothers Karamazov*. Tr. Richard Pevear and Larissa Volokhonsky. New York: Vintage, 1991

Gustafson, Richard F. *Leo Tolstoy, Resident and Stranger: A Study in Fiction and Theology*. Princeton: Princeton UP, 1986.

Kamenka, Eugene. "Tolstoy, Leo." *Encyclopedia of Philosophy*. Vol. 8. New York: Macmillan, 1967: 147

(PSS) Толстой, Л. Н. *Полное собрание сочинений в 90 томах, академическое юбилейное издание*. Москва: Государственное издательство художественной литературы, 1928–58.

Tolstoy Sees Foolishness, and Writes: From *On Life* to *Fruits of Enlightenment*, and Back Again

Michael D. Gordin
Princeton University

Was it better or worse for him there, where he woke up after this real death? Was he disappointed, or did he find there exactly what he had expected? We will all soon find out.

— Leo Tolstoy, "Master and Man"[1]

Everyone who has an opinion on the matter knows that Tolstoy thought that spiritualism was ridiculous. Whenever spiritualism appears in his novels — in *Anna Karenina* and *Resurrection* — Tolstoy resolutely derides it, but derides it with a purpose: only suggestible and somewhat gullible characters (with the possible exception of Vronsky) are interested in séances, and they often base disastrous decisions on what mediums convey to them as messages from the other world.[2] There would be, it seems, nothing more to say on the matter. Except that Tolstoy apparently needed to make this point about spiritualism over and over again. Why, if spiritualism was so foolish, did he repeatedly return to the topic? When we take Tolstoy's attention to spiritualism seriously — not necessarily spiritualism itself, but the writer's focus on it — it provides some missing connections between his art, his philosophy, and his religious conceptions.

Tolstoy had been aware of spiritualism from his voluminous reading — and even participated in some séances — from the very dawn of the European movement, even before it arrived in Russia, and he formed his dismissive attitude early. So one is surprised to learn that Tolstoy went to another séance in Moscow around 1886, and that the experience was so unsettling (or frustrating, or amusing?) for him that he immediately sketched a play on the subject. Almost contemporaneous with *The Kreutzer Sonata*, this sketch grew into one of his major literary products of the 1880s, entitled *The Fruits of Enlightenment*, a work that has been mostly overlooked as a source for the cultural context of Russian Spiritualism. The play is superficially a satire on the nobility, but the most prominent plot device animating this story of good-hearted peasants justly outwitting their silly betters is a faked spiritualist séance. I propose to take this comedy about a relatively marginal issue in Russian culture (spiritualism) and demonstrate its embedding in a unified vision of science, philosophy, and religion.

I situate *Fruits of Enlightenment* not among Tolstoy's dramatic works, or even among his fictional creations, but instead put this manifestly frivolous work in the context of *On Life* (*О Жизни*), Tolstoy's most highbrow and thorough philosophical writing. This is not a fanciful linkage. Tolstoy began *Fruits of Enlightenment* at almost exactly the same time as *On Life*, and set the play aside to produce what he later declared one of his two most important works.[3] When he finally resumed the dramatic sketch, he altered the play to emphasize satirizing spiritualist *scientists* (as opposed to its earlier emphasis on dilettante noble spiritualists). Ilya Vinitsky has already produced an excellent study of the play's professional hypnotist, Grossmann, in the context of Tolstoy's theory of art, arguing that hypnosis as a model for communication was a central concern for Tolstoy during this period of his life (Vinitsky 2009, 136–155). I shall instead focus on the "professor" in the story, Krugosvetlov. If we examine this figure carefully, especially his one big moment — an extended lecture on spiritualist theory — we find a series of themes that draw directly from Tolstoy's encounters with spiritualists and the ideas expressed in *On Life*, themes that will force us to reconsider the marginality of the spiritualist fad in the major religious thought of the mature writer.

What Is Spiritualism?: The Movement Arrives in Russia, and Stays

As an avid reader of the European press, Tolstoy became familiar with spiritualism in its early days of the 1850s. The movement itself was born in upstate New York in 1848, and spread quickly to Britain and then across the European continent.[4] We know that he encountered it personally in Paris, attending a séance lead by the outstanding Victorian medium Daniel Dunglas Home (pronounced "Hume"), the only medium from the epoch who was never publicly exposed as a fraud. On 16 March 1867, Tolstoy noted in his diary: "Hume both succeeded and didn't succeed (и сделал и не сделал). I must try it myself" (*PSS* 17:724).[5] (As far as we are aware, Tolstoy never made good on this promise.) Tolstoy was prescient in selecting Home: not only was he reportedly able to levitate and hold burning coals on his palms with no damage, but he had been the reason why the distinguished British chemist William Crookes, in attempting to debunk Home's miracles, became a committed spiritualist. Home also visited Russia on several occasions and married into a distinguished Russian family. His case alone thus demonstrates some crucial themes for this essay: the transition from Europe to Russia, the link between science and spiritualism, and Tolstoy's deep personal interest in both these issues.

Spiritualism should not be confused with a general interest in spirituality, or as an opposition to "materialism" (whatever that might mean). In this essay, spiritualism (Russian спиритизм, derived from the French *spiritisme*) refers to the practices that took place at séances. These were small gatherings of individuals — usually fewer than ten people — who assembled in a darkened room with a particular individual (the "medium") who could produce a variety of phenomena: table rappings, levitation of furniture, ringing of bells without human contact, automatic writing, etc. Just how these effects were produced was the source of much contemporary debate: for more mystically inclined spiritualists these were communications from the spirit world; for more scientistic ones they were interactions between psychic energy and matter; and for skeptics they were outright fraud. Anything was possible during the height of Russian spiritualism in the 1870s — except to be without an opinion.

Tolstoy began to engage spiritualism in writing during the 1875–1876 "spiritualist season." *Anna Karenina*, for example, was serialized in the *Russian Herald* (*Русский Вестник*) alongside many of the articles in that flurry of contestation (and features the medium Jules Landau, a fictionalized Home, whose appearance is well analyzed by Donna Orwin [Orwin 2004, 125]). The controversy of that year was prompted by an April 1875 article in defense of spiritualism, published in the *Messenger of Europe* (*Вестник Европы*), penned by Nikolai Petrovich Vagner. Vagner was an interesting man. A trained entomologist, he has been credited with the discovery of pædogenesis — the parthenogenetic reproduction of insect larvae — and he occupied with distinction the chair of zoology at both Kazan University and, starting in the 1870s, St. Petersburg University. Shortly after moving to the capital, he was drawn, despite much skepticism, to attend a few séances upon the invitation of Aleksandr Butlerov: academician, professor of chemistry at St. Petersburg University, and one of the most distinguished scientists in the Russian Empire. Vagner's curiosity was piqued, and 1875 he was converted. In addition to his spiritualist activities, he also penned a series of fairy tales (under the pseudonym Kot-Murlyka: (Кот-Мурлыка), "Cat Purr"), some of the finest non-naturalist writing produced in the Empire.[6] Vagner and Tolstoy knew each other as writers, and he appeared in many of the latter's letters under the derogatory moniker "Wurst," i.e. German sausage.

Vagner was soon joined publicly by Butlerov. The latter's scientific prominence and reputation for probity served to bolster the intellectual respectability of spiritualism after he entered the journalistic fray later in 1875. His support, and Vagner's, prompted their university colleague Dmitrii I. Mendeleev (most famous today for his 1869 formulation of the periodic system of chemical elements) to empanel a commission to ostensibly "investigate," but actually debunk, the claims of scientific spiritualists. These disputes were highly public in the 1870s, and Tolstoy, for one, took note of them.

Medium and Man: Tolstoy among the Spiritualists (and the Scientists)

When Tolstoy bothered to address spiritualism directly, Nikolai Strakhov (1828–1896) was usually involved. Trained in the natural sciences, Strakhov worked as a journalist and collaborator with Fedor Dostoevsky's journal *Time* (*Время*) (although he later slandered the novelist after his death) and eventually as a general conservative intellectual gadfly. From the 1870s on, he became close to Tolstoy, corresponding on a variety of topics and making frequent trips to Yasnaya Polyana. Despite the fact that he regretted Strakhov's unwillingness to devote himself to a religious life, Tolstoy clearly respected the latter's views on many topics, especially scientific ones.[7] In order to approach Tolstoy's understanding of spiritualism, therefore, we must begin with science; in particular, it is important to underscore that Tolstoy's hostility to spiritualism was not a manifestation of some "anti-scientific" attitude on his part. For Tolstoy was, properly speaking, not opposed to science at all.

This does not mean science was unproblematic. Although, like most members of the Russian intelligentsia of mid-century, he read widely in popular journals in both Russian and other languages about the tremendous developments in various fields — he was particularly taken with the work of Michael Faraday and James Joule — he remained suspicious of research in cell theory and microbiology, and (along with Strakhov) nurtured an abiding hostility to atomism.[8] Tolstoy's interest in science apparently stemmed from his general obsession with forms of method, definition, and (crucial for us) epistemology. While working on his important essay "What Is Art?," for example, Tolstoy wrote to Strakhov on 6 February 1891 demanding a definition of science:

> It's too long to write about, but I'd like to talk to you about it: in fact I'd like answers to these questions: (1) Does science, whose distinguishing feature is the strict verification of its propositions — criticism — apply this criticism to those propositions on the basis of which certain knowledge and information

is separated off from the whole infinite quantity of knowledge transmitted by people from generation to generation? (2) Can those features which constitute the special nature of scientific knowledge according to existing definition, be applied to knowledge of any kind — the most worthless and even harmful? (3) Is the distinguishing property of science the special nature of its content, not its form? (4) If there is any knowledge which is separated off by its content from all other knowledge as being especially important and meriting the special respect which is characteristically ascribed to science, is true art also distinguished by this same content from art which is not true? (reproduced in Tolstoy 1978, II:476)

It is clear from this statement (and there are others) that labeling Tolstoy "hostile" to science is an oversimplification. To some extent, this characterization has its roots in the common belief that science and religion are inexorably opposed, and since it goes without saying that Tolstoy was "religious," he must have been anti-scientific. This caricatures both the nuanced relationship of science and religion found in the history of science and Tolstoy's religious belief. One would be on far stronger grounds to view the writer as fascinated by the scientific project (as he understood it), and concerned to demarcate the proper domain for this powerful form of intellectual inquiry.

Precisely Tolstoy's worry over the proper domain of science — and the tendency of his contemporaries to ascribe to science too much *moral* power and too broad a social significance — accounts for his several reservations about the scientific endeavor, of which I will briefly mention three that exhibit characteristic features.[9]

First, Tolstoy repeatedly condemned contemporary medicine, particularly when physicians endorsed sexual activity as necessary for health (notably in *The Kreutzer Sonata*). He claimed that patients tended to deify doctors and outsource moral decision-making to them.[10] Second, and related, were Tolstoy's criticisms of Dmitrii I. Mendeleev's vision of transforming Russia into an industrial capitalist state, powered by a massive expansion of the Russian population. Based as it was on the birth of many more children — and thus a great deal more sex — Tolstoy declared the chemist's views "[h]orribly absurd" (*PSS* 55:237) in a diary entry of 24 August 1906, while reading Mendeleev's popular economic tract *To a Knowledge of Russia* (*К Познанию России*), a view he reiterated in letters and comments that summer while he was immersed in the book.[11]

The third prominent case was Tolstoy's famously negative view of Darwinism. Darwin's theories were widely available in Russia almost as soon as they were published, and the intelligentsia had access to both the scientific works and their popularizations. *The Origin of Species* was translated into Russian in 1864 by S. Rachinsky, with a second edition in 1865; noted physiologist I. M. Sechenov translated *The Descent of Man* in 1871, the same year as the English edition, with a second edition in 1874; *Variation of Animals and Plants*, *The Expression of the Emotions*, and *The Voyage of the Beagle* all appeared in the 1870s; and between 1907 and 1909 botanist K. A. Timiriazev ("Darwin's Russian Bulldog") oversaw an edition of eight volumes of Darwiniana in Russian. Criticism of Darwin's views from Russian naturalists stemmed mostly, as Daniel Todes has shown, from their belief that the Englishman had overemphasized Malthusian overpopulation and competition to the extent of ignoring cooperative trends in evolution.[12] Most of the reactions from members of the intelligentsia, however, were broadly in favor of the general tenor of Darwin's vision of nature.

The exceptions were conservatives, especially Nikolai Strakhov and Nikolai Danilevskii, who attacked the theory for being corrosive of morals. Tolstoy reacted similarly, although not as vehemently. At staggered points in the 1870s, especially in *Anna Karenina*, Tolstoy lashed out at Social Darwinist views that interpreted society as exhibiting the survival of the fittest, but he soon ceased to write on the matter. Unlike many other writers with strong views on evolution, he let Charles Darwin's death in 1882 pass without public comment, and he only became re-energized on the matter in 1885, when Strakhov began to polemicize on behalf of Danilevskii's massive posthumous volume *Darwinism*, and drew his famous friend into the fray. Tolstoy began to write more openly and frequently about the threat Darwinism posed to a religious life, but even here, as Hugh McLean has noted, Tolstoy's views shared the two central characteristics of his other wary views of modern science and medicine: Darwin's was a theory of the past, and thus had no bearing on what we must do *now*; and society as a whole misunderstood this and ascribed moral weight to these views, which distracted them from proper living. After about 1890 Tolstoy's views had solidified on this issue and he remained staunchly critical of Social Darwinism, without any nuance to differentiate the naturalist and sociological interpretations.[13]

Strakhov brought Tolstoy into the Darwinism fight, and he also inducted him into his campaign against séances and mediums, especially when endorsed by natural scientists like Butlerov and Vagner, which he objected to largely as a transgression against correct metaphysical reasoning. Strakhov dashed off a series of critical pieces attacking the metaphysics of mediumism in late 1876, after the bulk of the fury surrounding the Mendeleev commission had already subsided.[14] He had earlier sounded out Tolstoy's views on the matter, and the latter responded on 1–2 January 1876 with a long and surprising letter that reflected substantial preoccupation with both the epistemological and social issues posed by spiritualism:

> Second, I was struck by new proofs of our intellectual commonality. You write about spiritualism, I had almost written about it. My article is entirely ready. The article in the *Russian Herald* worried me terribly. Three things struck me. 1) That the muzhiks see devils incessantly, and no one considers this to be a phenomenon which deserves attention, that these are facts; but Butler and Wurst [Butlerov and Vagner – MG] see them, and I should believe them — these are facts. I would like to show that the case of the muzhiks' devils is just as authentic as theirs, but that Butler and Wurst don't deserve our trust, having become stupid by sitting over

> microscopes and retorts, but instead the fresh muzhik,
> who knows a great deal less (in your terms, his analysis
> is less developed), yet has the foundations of all knowl-
> edge — faith, a religious worldview (synthesis, if you
> like) that is without comparison more correct than
> Wurst's. (*PSS* 62:235–36)

Frustratingly for the historian, Tolstoy never drafted his "entirely ready" article. However, among his papers and scribbles, one finds related notes from October 1875 written in reaction to a pro-spiritu-alist piece. The thoughts here echo the above letter to Strakhov, and demonstrate how tightly Tolstoy wove the shenanigans at séances with his emerging philosophical worries that would blossom in his 1879 *Confession*:

> Observation, experiment, facts, inductive method. —
>
> Inductive, deductive — these are only words relat-
> ing to the essence of thinking. This difference and
> opposition makes sense only relating to the essence of
> thought. I.e., I can prove or express something induc-
> tively or deductively, but the thought occurs to me,
> it appears neither inductively nor deductively. And
> therefore it is impossible to produce a thought induc-
> tively. In order to make experiments, it is necessary to
> already have a *goal* for the experiments, in order to see
> facts, one must see what they prove. Phenomena such
> as mediumism only prove the poverty of thought of the
> people who affirm the med[iums]. The goal in mind
> during the experiments of mediumism is a thought.
> And this thought is superstition — i.e., the absence of
> a rational worldview. (*PSS* 17:724)

That is where Tolstoy left his views on spiritualism during the great year of public debate over Spiritualism — as private notes soon dis-missed, peripheral to his line of thought.

What Does Man Laugh By?: *Fruits of Enlightenment*

And then, for no discernible reason, Tolstoy's interest in the topic reawakened in the mid-1880s. Tolstoy's friend N. V. Davydov, having arrived in Moscow from Tula while the Tolstoys were visiting the metropole, heard from an acquaintance that N. A. L'vov, a respected nobleman and an avid amateur spiritualist, would be having a séance in a few days. Knowing that Tolstoy "wanted to participate at some point in such a séance, in order to convince himself with his own eyes in the imaginariness of everything that happened there," Davydov arranged for both of them to attend L'vov's séance (*TVS*, II: 205). We have no idea why Tolstoy evinced such an interest, but we do know his mind was just about made up. He told Davydov, as the latter recalled, "that he was surprised that people could believe in the reality of spiritualist phenomena; after all it is just the same, he said, as believing that if I strike my walking stick milk will flow from it, which has never happened and never will." (*TVS*, II: 205). Present at the event were Tolstoy, Davydov, L'vov, the medium (a man named Mamchich), P. F. Samarin, and K. Iu. Milioti. The séance was unsuccessful: everyone sat around a circular table in a dark room; there were knocks on the table and phosphorescent glows; Samarin brushed against a hand in the darkness; and then the medium came to. Afterwards, L'vov displayed some spiritualist photographs, and everyone retired. The next day, Davydov noted, Tolstoy "affirmed to me his opinion that in spiritualism everything is either self-deception, in which both the medium and the participants in the séance are complicit, or simply a deception created by professionals" (*TVS*, II:205). We do not know precisely when this happened, but the *terminus ante quem* is 1887, since L'vov died that year.

This single event was the trigger for Tolstoy's only creative work which devoted substantial attention to spiritualism, his comedy *The Fruits of Enlightenment*, which George Steiner delightfully dubbed "Tolstoy's *Meistersinger*, his one major excursion into gaiety" (Steiner, 129). It is obvious that the original sketch of the play (*PSS* 27:433–435) was directly inspired by the séance, since the names of the characters remain those of the original participants, especially L'vov and Samarin. (These are changed to Zvezdintsev and Sakhatov in the final version of the play.) The original sketch had the role of a "professor" — although none was present at the L'vov séance — and he was originally dubbed "Kutler," patently a *portmanteau* of Butlerov and Vagner. Kutler would eventually become Krugosvetlov, and his role was expanded when Tolstoy extensively revised the play in 1889. Although the play was drawn from real life, Tolstoy continued to develop the characters as he tinkered, transmuting them into literary creations that transform the play into more than merely a *roman à clef.*[15]

The timing of the first sketch of *Fruits of Enlightenment* places it immediately after the completion of *The Power of Darkness* (November 1886), but Tolstoy made little progress, achieving only a skeleton of acts one and two. The idea for the play was soon consigned to a drawer — displaced by the composition of *On Life* — and was only revived in 1889 due to a Jane Austenesque desire on the part of the young folks at Yasnaya Polyana to put on a play. The story comes to us from the reminiscences of A. M. Novikov, who was visiting Yasnaya Polyana in late 1889 and over a meal had a conversation with Tolstoy's daughter Maria, and the two came to the idea of staging a play. She turned to Novikov and said: "Haven't you read papa's play?" He assumed she meant *The Power of Darkness*, but she insisted upon "another one. I saw it among his papers" (*TVS* II:448). He asked her to obtain a copy, and this operation took a few days. The draft, which he recalled being titled "The Thread Has Snapped" (Ниточка оборвалась), was only a pale shadow of what would eventually be *Fruits of Enlightenment.*

Novikov immediately noticed the satire of the local nobility within it, however, and they decided to put on the play and apportioned the roles. Tolstoy at first objected that this kind of theater was an idle amusement of the rich — a somewhat strange criticism from the author of the farce — but he eventually acquiesced, even attending rehearsals and working seriously on corrections and revisions. Novikov and Maria summoned friends from Moscow, Tula, and Chern' to take part, and the production was staged on 30 December 1889. Tolstoy seemed to enjoy the whole process immensely, in particular V. M. Lopatin's portrayal of the third peasant.[16]

That is the standard account. Tolstoy did not actually abandon the play from 1886 to late 1889, only revived by the antics of the young adults. He had returned to the play after completing *On Life*, and he spent much of the spring of 1889 expanding the sketches until it reached the stage of the draft Mariia Lvovna Tolstaya filched from his writing desk, publishing it in 1891. The final revisions, after the success of the amateur theatricals, left Tolstoy uncomfortable, as one can see from a letter to his chief disciple V. G. Chertkov, dated 15 January 1890:

> Recently the comedy which was performed at home has so taken hold of me that I've been working on it continually over 10 days, improving it and embellishing it from an artistic point of view. The result is still a very insignificant and feeble work, but the thing is that it made me see what a soul-degrading occupation art is. A man may die at any time, and all of a sudden he jots down anxiously a phrase which is appropriate to a particular person and is funny; and he's glad to have found it. Generally speaking I felt ashamed, but I think I've finished now. (Tolstoy 1978, II:451)

Partly at issue here was Tolstoy's ambivalent attitude toward the theater, as George Steiner has analyzed well (Steiner, 116–117). But more relevant for us is Tolstoy's attention to the morally problematic nature of *comedy*, especially when writing parts suited to particular individuals. This applies directly to the character of Krugosvetlov.

Despite my emphasis on him, the professor was certainly not the main character. *The Fruits of Enlightenment* was essentially a classic farce, in which a smart peasant girl (Tania), manages to win her somewhat hapless lover (the kitchen boy Semyon), and persuade her noble master, Leonid Fedorovich Zvezdintsev, to sell land to Semyon's village family at reasonable rates. The rub is how Tania pulls this off. Zvezdintsev was an avid Spiritualist, and Tania rigs a séance by persuading him that Semyon, while napping, has mediumistic powers, and then "materializing" the deed of sale during the séance. There are other plot lines as well — the arrogant valet Grigorii who continually paws at Tania; the obsessive crusade of the lady of the house against germs and microbes, especially when spread by peasants (a thinly veiled and ruthless portrait of Tolstoy's wife); and so on — but none of these rise to the dominance, either structurally or thematically, of the staged séance.

Aside from Tania — and even she is a bit of a schemer — no one comes off well: the nobility are ninnies, the servants are feckless, and the peasants are shallow. Tolstoy himself later almost recanted both the content of the play and the practice of playwriting:

> In *Fruits of Enlightenment* I was, as the author, on the side of the peasants, but on stage suddenly they appeared to be the same kind of swindlers and cheats, like Grossmann, and conscious cheats at that. I can't reproach the actors for this — they performed well.... I understood from this that it is one thing to write, another to put on a play; there is a big difference between text and performance. (qtd. in Опульская, 259; ellipses added)

But perhaps no one is so irredeemably comic, so worthy of relentless mockery as the "Professor," Aleksei Vladimirovich Krugosvetlov, described in the dramatis personae as: "Scientist, 50 years of age, with calm, pleasantly self-assured manners and a sort of slow, singing speech. Speaks guardedly. He relates meekly and disdainfully to those who do not agree with him. Smokes a great deal. A thin, mobile person" (*PSS* 27:95). He is the figure that concentrates our attention on spiritualism itself with his smug all-knowing air in the midst of rank fraud.

Krugosvetlov is a pure "type": the scientist who has converted to a whole-hearted — but still scientific — belief in mediumistic phenomena, alongside such well-known British luminaries as William Crookes and Alfred Russel Wallace, both of whom were cited in the draft (*PSS* 27:112). Their Russian counterparts, Butlerov and Vagner, were not explicitly invoked, but the allusion was overt, even if Krugosvetlov was no longer named "Kutler." There are a few characteristics of this type which stood out to contemporaries, and which Tolstoy deftly satirized: an enthusiasm for explaining everything through the transformations of energy (*PSS* 27:185); the denial of spiritualist phenomena as "supernatural," but rather framing them as natural laws not yet fully understood (*PSS* 27:191–192); and the refusal to accept evidence of fraud by mediums, even when publicly confronted with the deception (*PSS* 27:246–247). (In the first draft of the play, after Semyon's fraud is exposed, the professor still wants to take the young man to Petersburg for further study [*PSS* 27:434].) Instead of providing many snippets of Krugosvetlov's mode of reasoning, I will instead reproduce Krugosvetlov's extremely long disquisition on the science behind spiritualism, which Tolstoy had expanded substantially for the final version of the play. The speech is not quite a monologue, as it is interrupted by giggles from the peanut gallery of flirting teenagers in the séance room, and by requests from the host to cut it short — all highly comic interventions designed to deflate any residual respect for the professor — but Krugosvetlov soldiers on:

> Gentlemen! The phenomenon which we study appears ordinary on the one hand, like nothing new, and on the other hand like something which is beyond the order of natural conditions. Neither the one nor the other is correct. This phenomenon is not new, but as old as the world, and is not supernatural, but is entirely subject to the same eternal laws to which everything existing is subject. This phenomenon is often described as communion with the spiritual world. This description is inexact. In this description the spiritual world is placed in opposition to the material world, but this is not correct: there is no such opposition. Both worlds are so tightly intercalated, that there is no possibility of setting a demarcation line which separates one world from the other. We say: matter is composed of molecules... [interruption] Molecules from atoms, but atoms, not having extension, are in essence nothing other than points of attachment of force. That is, strictly speaking, not force but energy — the same

energy which is just as uniform and indestructible as matter. But since matter is one, but its forms are diverse, just the same with energy. Until recently we knew only four forms of energy which can transform into each other: dynamic, thermal, electrical, and chemical. But four forms of energy are far from exhausting all the variety of its appearances. The forms of energy's appearance are multiple, and one of these new, little-known forms of energy is being studied by us. I am speaking of the energy of mediumism. [interruption] Mediumistic energy has been known to humanity from long ago: foresight, precognition, clairvoyance, and many others — all this is nothing more than a manifestation of mediumistic energy. The phenomena produced by it have been known for a long time. But the energy itself was not recognized as such until very recently, until one had recognized that medium, the vibrations of which produce mediumistic energy. And just as the phenomenon of light was unexplained until the existence of an imponderable substance, the ether, was recognized, just so mediumistic phenomena appeared mysterious until one recognizes the truth, now indubitable, that in the interstices of the ether particles there is another imponderable substance, still finer than the ether, which is not subject to the law of three dimensions... [interruption] And just as mathematical calculations confirmed incontrovertibly the existence of the imponderable ether that produces the phenomena of light and electricity, just so the brilliant array of most accurate experiments by Hermann Schmidt and Joseph Schmatzofen without doubt confirms the existence of that substance, which fills the universe and can be called the spiritual ether. [interruption] And thus, an array of strictly scientific experiments and researches, which I have the honor of informing you about, have clarified for us the laws of mediumistic phenomena. These experiments have clarified for us that the submersion of some persons in the hypnotic state, which differs from ordinary sleep only in that with the submersion in this sleep physiological activity not only doesn't decline, but always intensifies, as we just saw — it turns out, that the submersion in this state of whichever subject invariably entails certain perturbations in the spiritual ether, perturbations completely similar to those which are produced by the submersion of a solid body in a liquid. These perturbations are what we call mediumistic phenomena... [interruption]. (*PSS* 27:209–211; ellipses in the original)

Much revealing material lies buried here amid the obfuscation. Of course, there are echoes of some of the classic spiritualist tropes (transformations of energy, etc.). In a formal sense, the speech becomes increasingly abstract the more he is interrupted, exemplifying the detachment of Krugosvetlov from his immediate surroundings. But, most obviously, the entire passage is nothing more than a circular definition of "mediumistic phenomena." One analysis of Tolstoy's theater interprets this speech as an Aesopian critique of the dogmas of the established church, and there is merit to that argument.[17] My point, however, concerns not so much the content as why Tolstoy bothered to include such an extended speech in the play in the first place. It was not present, even as a placeholder, in the early drafts from 1886 or in such an extended form until the final version. The answer stems, I argue, from what intervened between the L'vov séance and the Yasnaya Polyana production: the writing of *On Life*.

How Much Science Does a Man Need?: *On Life*

On Life comprises perhaps the most complete statement of Tolstoy's epistemological and metaphysical views outside an explicitly religious frame, and it was composed at a crucial moment in his intellectual development — right after the break from Orthodoxy, and before his more explicit political radicalization. Tolstoy himself considered the work to be seminal, and yet aside from several incisive Russian reviews of the French translation of the text, it was soon broadly ignored.[18] For example, in 1890 it was considered completely responsible, in a survey article on contemporary trends in Russian philosophy, to declare that "[n]either Count Tolstoi nor his followers have any interest whatever in philosophy; they are even indifferent to ethics as a science" (Moki-evsky, 159). Even a cursory acquaintance with this text would disabuse anyone of such a gross oversimplification.

On Life represents a further stage in Tolstoy's decades of wrangling with problems of epistemology (evident in his philosophical fragments of 1847), the privileged role of nature in the formation of the self, and especially a confrontation with the pessimistic depiction of the will in the thought of Arthur Schopenhauer.[19] The central argument of the text, echoed in a comment buried in Appendix III, is that "Man always knows through reason, and not through faith. One might dissimulate, maintaining that he knows through faith and not through reason; but as soon as a person knows two faiths and sees people who profess a different faith than his own, then he is confronted with the inevitable necessity to decide the issue with reason" (*PSS* 26:439). For our purposes, it suffices to follow two of the main strands of argumentation: the rejection of the primary claimant to the power of reason in contemporary society — that is, science; and the application of the process of reason to resolve certain questions about the nature of suffering, theodicy, and the soul.

First, to science. Tolstoy maintained that the problem with science, at least at the epistemological level, was not its insistent commitment to rationalism (that was Dostoevsky's position), but rather its application of that rationalism to inappropriate problems. He had already articulated this view explicitly in an unpublished draft entitled "A Conversation on Science," drafted in 1875–1876, not coincidentally during the spiritualism controversies:

> Earlier science did not distance itself from the philosophical questions connected with it; now History says directly that questions of the purpose of humanity,

of the laws of its development are outside of science. Physiology says that it knows the path of activity of nerves, but questions about the freedom or lack thereof of a person are beyond its domain. Jurisprudence says that it knows the history of the emergence of these or those ordinances, but that the question of to which degree these ordinances answer to our idea of justice are beyond its domain, etc. Even worse, medicine says: your illness is outside of science. So what the devil do I care for your sciences? I'm better off playing chess. (*PSS* 17:141)[20]

Notice here that Tolstoy was most vexed with the historical and social sciences, well within the purview of наука, the Russian term that mirrors the German *Wissenschaft*. Distinctive about *On Life* was his extension of the analysis to the physical sciences through scientists' rampant abuse of reductionist reasoning.

The crux here, related to his critique of Darwinism, was the application of scientific theories to humans. Science proved unable to address the complexity posed by humanity:

[E]xamining man as a subject of observation we see, scientists say, that he eats this way, grows, reproduces, ages and dies, like all other animals.... For this we will examine the life of animals and plants in general. Examining these animals and plants, we see that in these still simpler laws of matter appear in common with both.... We see that what happens in the plant and the animal happens exactly the same way in man, they say, and thus we conclude that everything that happens in man is explained to us from what happens in the simplest dead matter visible to us.... The conception that in man there is something that we don't see either in plants, or in animals, or in dead matter, and that this something is the only subject of knowledge, without which all other forms are useless, doesn't trouble them. (*PSS* 26:350–351; ellipses added)

The tendency of contemporary scientists to search for uniformity in laws and regularity of phenomena — not unrelated to Krugosvetlov's mode of reasoning — meant they defined "science" in such a way as to exclude all the phenomena that not only made humanity unique, but were in fact the only questions worth posing. This inverted the proper order of philosophical reasoning, according to Tolstoy: "It is not the case that what we call science determines life, but our conception of life determines that which we should recognize as science. And thus, in order that science should be science, one must first of all resolve the question of what is and isn't science, and for this one must clarify the concept of life" (*PSS* 26:321).

This immediately raises the issue of which kind of knowledge — one may call it наука (science) if one likes — would be appropriate for the correct concept of life. Tolstoy spends most of *On Life* outlining an understanding of life consistent with his religious views (the divinity in all humanity and the obligation to build the Kingdom of God on Earth) and his political views (non-resistance to violence). The interconnection of these views is very intricate, and I will leave it to the other essays in this volume to do full justice to it. One point of relevance to my argument bears stressing, however: Tolstoy's explicit articulation of what happens after death. The answer? As far as we know, nothing — to the person who died. There is no evidence of any personal life after death. One of the crucial messages of *On Life* is that this fact is not a cause for fear:

> I will die. What's frightening in that? After all, how many various transitions have taken place and will take place in my bodily existence, and I do not fear them? Why should I fear this transition which has not yet happened and in which not only is there nothing repellent to my reason and experience, but which is so understandable, familiar, and natural for me, that in the continuation of my life I constantly made and

make judgments in which death, both of animals and of people, is taken by me as a necessary and often pleasant condition of my life. What's frightening about it? (*PSS* 26:398–399)

After death, individuals *do* in fact live on, but only in the memories of those who knew and loved them. The body is recycled by nature, and the "soul," still loved, moves beyond it. The critique here is not necessarily ontological (there is no afterlife), but is certainly epistemological (we have no knowledge of such an afterlife, and thus should not base our actions upon such expectations).[21] Fear of death is irrational; instead of focusing on a potentially non-existent afterlife, one should concentrate one's attentions on the present and living a life of love. The implication of this view for my argument should be clear: there is no evidence of a personal afterlife, one accessible to sense perception — Christian or spiritualist — and attempts to ponder it or (worse) communicate with it only distract from living in the here and now, building the Kingdom of God.

On Life thus embodies a critique of science that exactly mirrors the persona of Krugosvetlov — is, in fact, the philosophical justification of the creative satire present in *Fruits of Enlightenment* — but also importantly links a false understanding of reason within science to a pervasive fear of death. And this fear of death was precisely what made the spiritualists not just comic, but revelatory of a deep problem with the contemporary intelligentsia. One can see this connection in a shorter early draft of Krugosvetlov's monologue, where Tolstoy articulated the spiritualist credo thus: "The phenomenon is a communion with the invisible world. In this communion, whatever its form, there are two, always at least 2 factors. In the given case they are in general two: the human world, ours, corporeal, and the invisible, spiritual world" (*PSS* 27:466). The problematic move of splitting the world into present and absent halves is one of *the* central arguments of *On Life*. *Fruits of Enlightenment* was, from its earliest drafts on, an increasingly stylized expansion of his critique of science and its metaphysics, one refracted through actual representatives of the kind of scientist (and science) he rejected.

The Death of Aleksandr Butlerov: Tolstoy's Spiritualist Interlocutors

Despite his personal experiences with spiritualism — or perhaps because of them — Tolstoy was not very deeply informed about it. It is clear that during 1875 and 1876 he followed the articles on mediumistic phenomena published in the thick journals (it would have been hard to avoid those), but his library at Yasnaya Polyana contained nothing by Aleksandr Aksakov, Nikolai Vagner, Aleksandr Butlerov, or other major spiritualist writers.[22] The only important discussion of spiritualism he seemed to have read was *On Eternal Truths* (*О Вечных Истинах*), by Nikolai Strakhov, a book that includes a summary of the latter's hostile views on spiritualism. We know that he read this book carefully, and that he read it in February 1887 — that is, while composing *On Life*.[23]

While Tolstoy was thus exposed to spiritualism — attending séances, reading books — he also made it clear in a letter to Strakhov, probably from December 1885, commenting on Strakhov's most recent newspaper polemic against Butlerov (who died the following year), that he could not be bothered to care about spiritualism, and that Strakhov was approaching the issue the wrong way.[24] In this same letter, Tolstoy immediately transitioned into a mode of philosophical analysis that is strikingly reminiscent of *On Life*, implying that this would be the correct way (*PSS* 63:312–314). At each point we look, then, it seems that Tolstoy found spiritualism at an exact juncture with his philosophical system.

I emphasize that spiritualism is relevant in understanding Tolstoy's thought because he thought it was *unimportant*. Its marginality to his main line of thinking, his perception of it as a silly fad, is precisely why we can detect in his works the manifold interconnections between his philosophy, his religion, and his prose — akin to the technique of detecting art forgeries by looking at an earlobe, or the paw of a dog, rather than the supposedly distinctive eyes or the hands of the master being imitated.[25] But this marginality did not prevent those for whom spiritualism was central, such as Nikolai Vagner, from forcing Tolstoy to articulate some of the commitments explored above.

Their correspondence on *Fruits of Enlightenment* consists of three letters, and it is worth reproducing the first by Vagner and then Tolstoy's response *in toto* here. Vagner initiated the exchange with a letter to the Sage of Yasnaya Polyana on 22 March 1890:

> Deeply Esteemed Lev Nikolaevich!
>
> Yesterday I was at a meeting of the "Russian Literary Soc." and heard your comedy "*The Fruits of Enlightenment*." I went to hear this new work of yours, which was mentioned in "*New Time*." — I thought that much was misstated in this notice. — I said to myself: "It cannot be that a writer of such greatness, such enormous talent, Mr. Tolstoy wrote a libel (пасквиль) on professors, on scientists!["]
>
> To my great regret, it's true! It was painful and hard to hear that you with your usual artistic mastery razzed me and my friend, A. M. Butlerov.
>
> Several times during the reading I asked myself: is it perhaps hard for me because this mockery offends me personally or my dear departed friend? And I answered completely objectively: no!... It is hard for me because they are razzing the truth.
>
> Never until this moment since I have been a member of the Literary Soc. had a session been so well attended as yesterday. All the opponents of spiritualism came in order to hear your razzing of them. And all came to the conclusion that your razzing is just as talented as your writing of serious works.
>
> "Don't kick a prostrate man," say our people, on whose behalf you, entirely justly, advocate so fiercely. Spiritualism is a prostrate truth, forgotten and "disgraced by the enemy" (*Свет* 1877).

You found it necessary to add to all these insults also your own personal stamp. You achieved your goal. If someone from the Soc. remained halfway in contemplation, then he is now converted to your side — because there is nothing stronger than mockery. To the word of the Journal jokers and the Literary gaffers you have added your talented honest word.

You attack doctors with complete justification — you are completely right to accuse us scientists — in our egotistical and too-specialized strivings. But this is not your thought [alone]. Much earlier than you I said this in print. Here are my words: "It is necessary that scientists come down from the scientific heights and glance at the place which calls to them with one great principle, one great word, which vivifies and unifies everything. This great powerful word: humanity!"

In the name of this great word, I worked and work seriously in this area, about which you know nothing and which you, nevertheless, razz!

You preach not to resist evil with evil, and you yourself do evil. In our contemporary society laughter, and above all evil mockery, is the most powerful evil. Yesterday during the reading of your libel, I several times had to encounter and bear the double-meaning and mocking glances of my fellow members of the Literary Society. We spiritualists do not pay, cannot pay, evil for evil and can only from our whole souls wish you more talent and more strength for your works for the good of your land and your people.[26]

Tolstoy's response, a mixture of contrition and counter-accusation, followed on 25 March 1890:

Dear and truly respected Nikolai Petrovich*,

Your letter aroused the very feelings which you probably wanted to arouse by it — feelings of regret, remorse
almost, and grief that I caused distress, although unwit-
tingly, to a man I love and respect, and above all love
and gratitude to you for your loving attitude towards a
man who has caused you pain. Please forgive me first of
all and then hear me out. By way of justification I would
say the following: (1) that this comedy had been written by me a long time ago in rough and discarded; it
saw the light of day unexpectedly; my daughters asked
me if they could perform it, I began to revise it without
thinking it would get any further than our house and in
the end it was widely circulated. This is a feeble justification, but still it is one: if I had really thought of it for
publication, it's very possible I wouldn't have published
it as it is. (2) I never thought of you or Butlerov when
I was writing the comedy.[27] All that I knew of Butlerov
inspired my respect, and I've already told you of the
feelings I have for you. The professor is a personifica-
tion of a constantly encountered and comic contradiction: the profession of strict scientific methods and of
the most fantastic formulations and assertions. (3) —
And most important — is my loathing, which increases
with the years and which I don't disavow, for all superstitions, among which I reckon spiritualism. The more
I look at people's lives the more convinced I am that
the main obstacle to getting things done, or rather a
delaying factor, is the various superstitions which have
grown on to the true teaching from different sides, and
are preventing it from getting through to people's souls.
Superstitions are the spoonful of tar which ruins the
barrel of honey, and it's impossible not to hate them
or at least not to make fun of them. I recently visited
the Optina Monastery and saw people there burning with true love for God and mankind, and at the

same time considering it necessary to stand for several hours a day in church, take communion, and give and receive blessings, thereby paralysing the active power of life in themselves. I can't help hating these superstitions. I see how for some people these superstitions substitute the form for the essence, for others are an instrument of disunity, and for others again a means of repelling them from the true teaching. It's the same with any superstition, with any spoonful of tar. And the reason is that truth is common to all, universal, the property of all mankind, while superstitions are egotistical. Superstitions are particular forms, agreeable and convenient for particular people in particular situations. As soon as a man is in a different situation, other people's superstitions repel him and his superstitions repel them. Such in my opinion are the superstitions of all churches and such too are those of spiritualism. It seems to me that people who are followers of a particular kind of private teaching ought to learn to separate the truth common to all from what they alone, these particular people, consider to be the truth. If that were so, if they didn't consider that communion, or the origin of the holy spirit, or the existence of spirits were just as indisputable truths as the law of humility, unselfishness, or the purity of love, if they were to dissolve their spoonful of tar in a special vessel without infecting the whole barrel, it would be possible not to hate these private teachings. Then it would be possible to agree over those enormous areas which are common to all people, and not to touch on those areas which are distorted in such varied and fanciful ways in so many different creeds. I thought this particularly keenly when I read or heard about your work, deeply sympathetic to me, in the name of the principle of humanity which you mention in your letter. I constantly experience these feelings when I receive, as I have done recently, from America, a great many spiritualist publications and journals, many of which, for example *World's Advance Thought*, are filled with the highest Christian spirit.

This is my confession to you: please forgive me once again if in making it I have expressed myself too harshly anywhere. I will say, as children say: forgive me, it will be the first and last time; the last time because having once spoken my mind, I shall never speak to you about spiritualism again, and if you don't deprive me of friendship and communication with you, I shall only communicate with you about those areas where there is agreement between us. It seems to me that this is possible, and I hope that the circumstance which was the cause of this correspondence will not be the instrument of disunity, but on the contrary of rapprochement between us.

Yours truly and affectionately,

L. Tolstoy

* Forgive me if I have got your patronymic wrong. I could have found it out in town, but there is nowhere to do so in the country. (Tolstoy 1978, II:455–456; see the original in *PSS* 65:58–60)

Vagner, not taking Tolstoy's hint to drop the matter, responded with a final letter on 10 April 1890, which repeated many of the claims from the former, but at substantially greater length. After an extended opening in which he compared spiritualists to early Christians suffering for their beliefs, he turned back to the question of *Fruits of Enlightenment*, "which I consider (forgive my candor) an effort unworthy of a writer with such a broad, powerful talent, as yours is." He continued: "After all, we spiritualists have fewer enemies abroad than we have in Russia — and these enemies with full joy will now laugh and point their fingers at us. *Das ist Herr Seelig Prof Butlerow, und dass [sic] ist wanneritizig prof. Wagner!* Isn't this an evil thing that you have done?" Superstition does not enter the picture: "Your interpretation is contrary to the nature of the human soul which wants and thirsts for eternal life, eternal striving to the good and light." [28] And that, precisely, was what Vagner did not understand: the striving for eternal life was the very problem that Tolstoy was trying to eradicate. And it is for that reason that spiritualism was more important to him than he ever let on.

He did not respond to this second letter. According to the reminiscences of P. G. Ganzen, Tolstoy recalled this particular exchange with a certain amount of humor: "The beginning of the letter was good, friendly, but then the professor suddenly began to turn bitter and reproached me because I, a person that he so loves and esteems, allowed himself to so cruelly mock his dearest beliefs." Tolstoy in this recounting was more honest about the motivation for writing the comedy: it was not simply because his daughter wanted to perform something, but "because I thought it was necessary. I could perhaps have answered him and explained that this was only a misunderstanding from his side, but the tone of his letter was so irritating that I could not expect any positive result from my letter and thus I didn't answer him" (*TVS*, I:462–63). And thus the exchange ended, and mostly for the best. As Tolstoy wrote to V. G. Chertkov on 1 July 1890, after the dust had settled: "I'm very glad about Vagner — chiefly that he is not angry, but is good towards me" (*PSS* 87:32). All's well that ends well.

But nothing really ends for either the spiritualist or the Tolstoyan: for the former, the soul lives on (and maintains sporadic contact, under very specific and controlled conditions, with this world); and for the latter, it is love that persists. Beyond this merely formal parallel, there were clearly deeper connections between the modern spiritualists and Tolstoy's mature religious and philosophical thought — deny them though Tolstoy might. His irritation with mediumism burned for a long time, although admittedly on a very low flame. The question remains, however, as to why he was so bothered by it. It is difficult to formulate a concrete answer to this question without delving further into psychobiography than either evidence or inclination permits, but some tentative interpretations present themselves. Perhaps he disliked spiritualism because it proposed a voice beyond the grave, which, as Gary Saul Morson has suggested, was seen by Tolstoy (as in his drafted suicide note) to be a particularly powerful form of discourse — and thus he resented it (Morson, 27).[29] Or maybe the source was less aesthetic. Ilya Vinitsky suggests that "Tolstoy hated Modern Spiritualism because for him it represented a poor caricature (or a profanation) of his own deeply held beliefs" (Vinitsky 2009, 141). This seems closer to the mark, but a reading of *On Life* excludes this interpretation. If Tolstoy's philosophical (and religious) *oeuvre* leaves the reader with any single thought, it is that we are utterly ignorant of the afterlife, and thus can rationally expect no reward beyond what we do here and now.

The fact that only our present actions have any spiritual relevance for Tolstoy, that they are our only way of realizing the Kingdom of God, is not to be understood as resignedly settling for the present. For Tolstoy, the notion is much richer than quietism. These very actions in the present, these demonstrations of love, are precisely how the "soul" of the departed lives on with us. These actions are importantly not ritualized, not invested in a clerical-lay distinction, but are everyday acts of goodness. Spiritualism is thus entirely wrong-headed, and doubly so: first, it assumes the existence of a personal afterlife in order to explain the phenomena observed in séances, which perpetuates a paralyzing fear of death; and it does so through extensive rituals (darkened rooms, elaborate protocols) and specially designated intermediaries (mediums). No, spiritualism cannot be understood as a caricature of Tolstoyan principles.

But Tolstoy most definitely understood it as a caricature — not of his own views, but of every other established religion that preached the afterlife and mystical communion with the Godhead. Whereas in *Anna Karenina* or *Resurrection* spiritualism was a diagnostic probe used to expose the dim-wittedness and venality of the shallow St. Petersburg nobility, after *On Life* Tolstoy's references to spiritualism (with the partial exception of *Resurrection*) stake out deeper claims for the source of its wrongness. In "Religion and Morality," for example, an essay dated 28 October 1893 — and thus after both *On Life* and

Fruits of Enlightenment — Tolstoy dismissed spiritualism in passing in the following terms: "Modern spiritualism, which has as it foundation the preservation of individuality and its goodness, also flows from this attitude to the world. All pagan cults — divination, the idolization of those who enjoy themselves as men, or interceding saints, all sacrifices and prayers about the giving of earthly goods and the deliverance from evil — flow from this attitude to life" (*PSS* 39:9). Or, more explicitly and concretely, one finds in his diary entry of 29 December 1897:

> The spiritualists say that after death the soul of people lives on and communicates with them. Soloviev, the father, said truly, I remember that this is the Church dogma of saints, of their intercession and of prayers to them. Evgenii Ivanovich also said truly that as the Pashkov Sect is a taking out of the dogma of the Redemption alone and the adaptation of everything to it, so spiritualism is the taking out of the dogma of saints, and the adaptation of everything to it. (Tolstoy 1993, 188)

This, then, might be our answer as to why Tolstoy could not leave the séances alone: spiritualism was, to his mind, manifestly *silly*, and yet it served as a boiled-down, simplified outline of precisely what was wrong with mainstream Christianity: the clergy, the dogma, the rituals. These were things that distracted people from the true message of Christ. And that was no laughing matter.

(Notes)

1   I would like to thank Mikhail Dolbilov, Caryl Emerson, Inessa Medzhibovskaya, Leeore Schnairsohn, Ilya Vinitsky, and the participants in the April 2010 Princeton кружок for comments on an earlier draft of this essay. All dates are in the old-style Julian calendar, which lagged twelve days behind the Western European Gregorian calendar in the nineteenth century. Unattributed translations are my own.
     My translation. See the original in *PSS* 29:46.

2   For a presentation of this received view, see Berry, 86–87, and 93.

3   Tolstoy considered the other important work to be "What I Believe" (*В чем моя вера*), as documented in Опульская, 116.

4   The material that follows on the history of spiritualism is drawn from Chap. 4 in Gordin 2004, 84–112, and references therein. On spiritualism in Russia, see also Mannherz, who addresses the hostility of the Orthodox Church to the new movement — an important point I will bypass in this essay — on pages 6 and 17 of her dissertation.

5   Tolstoy wrote Home's name in Latin letters, spelling it according to its pronunciation; the misspelling is thus in the original. On Home, see Home 1863; Home 1878; and Jenkins.

6   For more detail on Vagner's career both in and outside science, see Gordin 2011. For an illuminating analysis of his spiritualism, see Chap. 4 in Vinitsky 2009, 89–106.

7   On the relationship between the two men, see Gerstein, 147–148; Medzhibovskaya, 161; and Orwin 2007. Tolstoy's occasional frustration with Strakhov should not be discounted, however. He once remarked to a friend: "Strakhov is like a piece of wood; you poke and poke with your finger at him, you think there will be something there, but no — your finger passes right through, where there is no texture — there is precisely no center in him, it is all eaten away by science and philosophy" (qtd. in Gerstein, 178).

8   See Orwin 1993, 188–189; and Medzhibovskaya, 139. To be fair to Tolstoy, although atomism was rapidly gaining ground among chemists and physicists across the nineteenth century, the theory still met significant opposition in scientific quarters. See Nye and Gordin 2004, 24–25.

9   I leave aside here the claim in Edgerton that Tolstoy's conception of space and time, especially as articulated in *On Life*, anticipated many of the discoveries of twentieth-century physics. This scientization of Tolstoy renders him even more of a prophet, forecasting developments in physics that were undreamt of when the Russian actually wrote. This approach differs from the far more successful attempt to situate Russian writers as reacting directly to their *contemporary* science, as Knapp does for Dostoevsky. See Knapp.

10   See Schefski. Tolstoy's reservations about physicians were doubled for specialists in mental health, but this did not prevent the emergence of a move-

ment within psychiatry to provide a "Tolstoyan" therapeutic experience. See the excellent analysis in Chap. 3 in Sirotkina, 74–116, who also discusses the many remote diagnoses, such as those by Cesare Lombroso and Max Nordau, of Tolstoy as mentally ill. Lombroso revised his opinion after actually meeting the Russian writer (Sirotkina, 79).

11 See Булгаков, I(ii):24. See also Tolstoy to Grand Duke Nikolai Mikhailovich, 25 April – 1 May 1902, in Tolstoy 1978, II:616. On Mendeleev's economic projects, see Chap. 6 in Gordin 2004, 145–174.

12 See Todes and Rogers.

13 For Tolstoy's views, see the very helpful analysis in McLean. On Danilevskii, see Данилевский; Тимирязев; and Фаминцын. Strakhov's opposition to Darwin can be seen, for example, in Страхов 1902.

14 See Страхов 1876a; Страхов 1876b; and Страхов 1876c.

15 See Опульская, 187; Полякова, 150–151; and Гудзий, 647–669, esp. 656.

16 See A. M. Novikov's account in *TVS*, I:448–50; P. A. Sergeenko's version in *TVS*, II:149; and V. M. Lopatin's blissfully self-satisfied rendition in *TVS*, II:96–100.

17 See Полякова, 179.

18 The reception is well discussed in Scanlan.

19 On the issues of epistemology and nature, see Gustafson, 212 and 221–222. On Schopenhauer, see Orwin 1993, 150; and McLaughlin.

20 For further discussion of this "Conversation," see Medzhibovskaya, 167–168.

21 Especially in his earlier writings, Tolstoy had relaxed some aspects of his ontological critique, although the epistemological resistance was always present. See the helpful analysis in Vinitsky 2010.

22 However, S. A. Bers noted in her reminiscences of Tolstoy that "[w]hen spiritualism became the fashion, Lev Nikolaevich visited the late professor Butlerov and was struck in astonishment at his belief in spiritualism" (*TVS*, I:187). If such an event ever took place (there is no corroboration), it would have to have been in the mid-1870s. Interestingly, Aleksandr Aksakov, the central figure of Russian spiritualism, wrote a review of *Resurrection*, which cited lengthy extracts from *On Life*, and appended Dostoevsky's critique of spiritualism. See Аксаков.

23 See Булгаков, I(ii):284.

24 The Countess disagreed. On 21 February 1884, she wrote to Strakhov in delight about his opposition to spiritualism: "I read your article in 'Novoe vremia' [New Time] with interest; who are Vagner and Comp[any] to polemicize with you!" (reproduced in Донсков, 171).

25 See Ginzburg.

26 Н. П. Вагнер Л. Н. Толстому, 22 марта 1890, ИРЛИ РАН f. 231, d. 279, ll. 1–3.

27 This is obviously false, since Tolstoy had originally named the character

of Krugosvetlov "Kutlerov" and then "Kutler," a compromise between Butlerov and Vagner.

28 Н. П. Вагнер Л. Н. Толстому, 10 апреля 1890, ИРЛИ РАН f. 231, d. 279,
ll. 4-9ob. The German in this letter is almost nonsensical; Vagner might be
parodying poor German speech.

29 To be very clear, Morson makes absolutely no connection between spiritualist messages and posthumous speech. The connection, however tenuous,
is mine.

Archival Credits

ИРЛИ РАН Институт Русской Литературы Российской Академии Наук
(Пушкинский Дом, Санкт-Петербург)

Works Cited

Аксаков, А. Н. *К чему было воскресать? По поводу романа графа Толстого
'Воскресенье'*. Санкт-Петербург: В. Демаков, 1900.

Berry, Thomas E. *Spiritualism in Tsarist Society and Literature*. Baltimore: Ed-
gar Allan Poe Society, 1985.

Данилевский, Н. И. *Дарвинизм: Критическое исследование*. Том 1. Часть
1. Санкт-Петербург: Меркурий Елизарович Комаров, 1885.

Донсков, А. А., *ред. Л. Н. Толстой и С. А. Толстая. Переписка с Н. Н.
Страховым*. Москва и Оттава: Славянская исследовательская группа
при Оттавском университете и Государственный музей Л. Н. Толстого,
2000.

Булгаков, В. Ф. *Библиотека Льва Николаевича Толстого в Ясной Поляне.
Библиографическое описание*, в 2-х томах. Москва: Книга, 1972-77.

Edgerton, William B. "Tolstoy, Immortality, and Twentieth-Century Physics."
Canadian Slavonic Papers 21 (September 1979): 289–300.

Фаминцын, А. С. "Н. А. Данилевский и дарвинизм: Опровергнут ли дарвинизм Данилевским?" *Вестник Европы* 24.2 (1889): 616–43.

Gerstein, Linda. *Nikolai Strakhov*. Cambridge, MA: Harvard UP, 1971.

Ginzburg, Carlo. *Clues, Myths, and the Historical Method*. Tr. John Tedeschi
and Anne C. Tedeschi. Baltimore: Johns Hopkins UP, 1992.

Gordin, Michael D. *A Well-Ordered Thing: Dmitrii Mendeleev and the Shadow
of the Periodic Table*. New York: Basic Books, 2004.

—. "Seeing Is Believing: Professor Vagner's Wonderful World." *Histories of Scientific Observation*. Ed. Lorraine Daston and Elizabeth Lunbeck. Chicago:
University of Chicago Press, 2011. 135–55.

Гудзий, Н. К. "'Плоды просвещения'. История писания и печатания
комедии 'Плоды Просвещения'." Толстой, Л. Н. *Полное собрание*

сочинений в 90 томах, академическое юбилейное издание. Том 27. Москва: Государственное издательство художественной литературы, 1936. 647–69.

Gustafson, Richard F. *Leo Tolstoy: Resident and Stranger: A Study in Fiction and Theology.* Princeton: Princeton UP, 1986.

Home, D. D. *Incidents in My Life.* London: Longman, Roberts & Green, 1863.

—. *Lights and Shadows of Spiritualism,* 2nd. ed. London: Virtue & Co., 1878.

Jenkins, Elizabeth. *The Shadow and the Light: A Defence of Daniel Dunglas Home, the Medium.* London: Hamish Hamilton, 1982.

Knapp, Liza. *The Annihilation of Inertia: Dostoevsky and Metaphysics.* Evanston, IL: Northwestern UP, 1996.

Л. Н. Толстой в воспоминаниях современников, в 2-х томах. под редакцией Г. В. Красновой, К. Н. Ломунова, С. А. Макашиной, Н. Н. Фортунатова и др. Москва: Государственное издательство художественной литературы, 1978 /abbreviated *TVS I* and *TVS II* where Romans indicate volume 1 or volume 2 of this edition/.

Mannherz, Julia. "Popular Occultism in Late Imperial Russia." Ph.D. Dissertation, University of Cambridge, 2005.

McLaughlin, Sigrid. "Some Aspects of Tolstoy's Intellectual Development: Tolstoy and Schopenhauer." *California Slavic Studies* 5 (1970): 187–245.

McLean, Hugh. "Claws on the Behind: Tolstoy and Darwin," *Tolstoy Studies Journal* 19 (2007): 15–32.

Medzhibovskaya, Inessa. *Tolstoy and the Religious Culture of His Time: A Biography of a Long Conversion, 1845–1887.* Lanham, MD: Lexington Books, 2008.

Mokievsky, P. K. "Philosophy in Russia." *Mind* 15 (1890): 155–60.

Morson, Gary Saul. *Hidden in Plain View: Narrative and Creative Potentials in "War and Peace."* Stanford: Stanford UP, 1987.

Nye, Mary Jo. "The Nineteenth Century Atomic Debates and the Dilemma of an 'Indifferent Hypothesis.'" *Studies in History and Philosophy of Science* 7 (1976): 245–68.

Опульская, Л. Д. *Лев Николаевич Толстой. Материалы к биографии с 1886 по 1892 год.* Москва: Наука, 1979.

Orwin, Donna. "Did Dostoevsky or Tolstoy Believe in Miracles?" *A New Word on The Brothers Karamazov.* Ed. Robert Louis Jackson. Evanston, IL: Northwestern UP, 2004. 125–141.

—. "Strakhov's *World as a Whole*: A Missing Link between Dostoevsky and Tolstoy." *Poetics. Self. Place: Essays in Honor of Anna Lisa Crone.* Ed. Catherine O'Neil, Nicole Boudreau, and Sarah Krive. Bloomington: Slavic Publishers, 2007. 473–93.

—. *Tolstoy's Art and Thought, 1847–1880.* Princeton: Princeton UP, 1993.

Полякова, Е. И. *Театр Льва Толстого. Драматургия и опыты ее прочтения.* Москва: Искусство, 1978.

Rogers, James Allan. "Russian Opposition to Darwinism in the Nineteenth Century." *Isis* 65 (1974): 487–505.

Scanlan, James P. "Tolstoy among the Philosophers: His Book *On Life* and Its Critical Reception." *Tolstoy Studies Journal* 18 (2006): 52–69.

Schefski, Harold K. "Tolstoj's Case against Doctors." *Slavic and East European Journal* 22 (1978): 569–73.

Sirotkina, Irina. *Diagnosing Literary Genius: A Cultural History of Psychiatry in Russia, 1880–1930.* Baltimore: Johns Hopkins UP, 2002.

Steiner, George. *Tolstoy or Dostoevsky: An Essay in the Old Criticism*, 2nd. ed. New Haven: Yale UP, 1996.

Страхов, Н. Н. "Дурные признаки." Н. Н. Страхов, *Критические статьи (1861–1894).* Под ред. И. П. Матченко. Том 2. Киев: Типография И. И. Чоколова, 1902: 379–97.

—. "Три письма о спиритизме. Письмо первое. Идолы." *Гражданин*, 15 ноября 1876, № 41–2: 981–3. [Abbreviated as Страхов 1876a]

—. "Три письма о спиритизме. Письмо второе. За непосвященных," *Гражданин*, 22 ноября 1876, № 43: 1015–8. [Abbreviated as Страхов 1876b]

—. "Три письма о спиритизме. Письмо третье. Границы возможного," *Гражданин*, 29 ноября 1876, № 44: 1056–9. [Abbreviated as Страхов 1876c]

Тимирязев, К. А. "Опровергнут ли дарвинизм?" *Русская мысль* 5 (май–июнь 1887): 145–80.

Todes, Daniel P. *Darwin Without Malthus: The Struggle for Existence in Russian Evolutionary Thought.* New York: Oxford UP, 1989.

(*PSS*) Толстой, Л. Н. *Полное собрание сочинений в 90 томах, академическое юбилейное издание.* Москва: Государственное издательство художественной литературы, 1928–58.

—. *The Journal of Leo Tolstoi (First Volume — 1895–1899).* Tr. Rose Strunsky. New York: Howard Fertig, 1993 [1917].

—. *Tolstoy's Letters.* Ed. and tr. R. F. Christian, 2 vols. London: Athlone Press, 1978.

Vagner, N. P. (Вагнер Н. П.) Н. П. Вагнер Л. Н. Толстому, 10 апреля 1890, ИРЛИ РАН f. 231, d. 279, ll. 4-9ob

Vinitsky, Ilya. *Ghostly Paradoxes: Modern Spiritualism and Russian Culture in the Age of Realism.* Toronto: University of Toronto Press, 2009.

—. "The Worm of Doubt: Prince Andrei's Death and Russian Spiritual Awakening of the 1860s." *Anniversary Essays on Tolstoy.* Ed. Donna Tussing Orwin. Cambridge: Cambridge UP, 2010. 120–37.

Notes on an Impersonal Life

Eugene Thacker
The New School

1.

Tolstoy's essay *On Life* begins with the most basic intuition: that life is contradictory. My life is not your life. And yet, both of us, as living, partake of something called "life" that is greater than my life or your life. Life is, above all, something that is *lived*, and as such, this living of life has the characteristic of something self-apparent and unquestionable about it. As Tolstoy notes early on in his essay, "[t]he word *life* is very short and very clear, and everybody knows what it means" (Tolstoy, 6). And yet, we as human beings also excel at thinking about life, whether it be in the concrete (my life, your life, this life) or in the abstract (the meaning of life, *media vita in morte sumus*, "in the midst of life we are death," and so on). "Life" seems to be split between the concrete instances of the living and a more general, more "philosophical" presupposition concerning something called "Life" that is common to each instance of the living.[1]

As conscious, reflective human beings we find ourselves in the predicament of being both inside and outside life, living life in the immersive continuity of its temporal flux and flow, and standing apart from life, studying it as one object among others in a world arrayed before our critical gaze. One might even say that one lives life at the expense of thinking about it. Furthermore, "life" becomes difficult to separate from the concept of "life," for while life pre-exists the concept of life, the concept of life—for human beings—makes possible a whole range of different ways of living life. "For the meaning of the word is clear to everyone not because it has been very accurately defined by other words and concepts, but on the contrary because it expresses a fundamental conception from which many others, if not all others, are deduced" (Tolstoy, 6).

As both a foundation and the confusion between concept and thing itself, life is registered as contradiction in our living it. Hence Tolstoy's almost Hobbesian formulation of "the fundamental contradiction of life" inhering in the relation between one life and another: "Having understood this, man sees that his personal welfare, in which alone he understands life, is not merely a thing not easy of attainment, but is something that will certainly be taken from him" (Tolstoy, 17).

2.

The intuition of life as contradictory is connected, for Tolstoy, to the variability in which we use the term, as well as to the multiple meanings the term has accrued in the modern era of biology, zoology, psychology, and medicine, not to mention the uses to which life is put in modern industrialism and mass media. Each one of these specialized fields attempts to get at the whole by examining in great detail a part. It is akin to the parable concerning a group of blind men examining an elephant. Each examines one part of the elephant only. When they compare notes with each other they find they are in complete disagreement.

3.

At first glance, religion appears to offer a solution to the contradictions of life. For Tolstoy, its solution is simple: to split life internally, between this life and another life, between living here and now and a deferred life after life. The internal split roughly corresponds to the split between science and religion, the life of the animal and the life of the spirit. Tolstoy sardonically gives them the names of the "Pharisees" and the "Scribes." The Pharisees, forever gazing up at the skies or just over the horizon, refusing the stink of the mud in which their feet are tentatively planted; and the Scribes, with their noses imperceptibly close to their instruments of measurement and calculation, stubbornly refusing any life that will not mould itself to the machinations of reason.

According to Tolstoy, both the Pharisees and the Scribes are deluded, though in different ways. The Pharisees, in their infinite deferral of life in another life (a life elsewhere, a life beyond, a life after), transform life into a ghostly shadow of itself. For the Pharisees, life is precisely that which is never lived (at least not now). By contrast, the Scribes, in their obsession with a principle of sufficient reason (a "principle of sufficient life" we might say), redefine life within the narrow confines of parameters that they themselves have concocted. For the Scribes, the height of instrumental reason is to have reduced intelligence to instinct, thought to brain activity, and the human to the animal.

As problematic as each approach may be, there is a strong pessimistic strand in the Pharisees and the Scribes. For both of them, there is a sense in which life is defined as that which is not worth living. The Pharisees conceive of earthly, animal life as unworthy and as empty of value, placing all their hopes in a life after life, while the Scribes do nearly the reverse, and conceive of any illusions or superstitions about life as unworthy, placing all of their attention on the animal life of blood, breath, and flesh, the life of eating and being eaten, the life that is the way-station between birth and death.

4.

The split, within life, between "this life" and "another life" is unique, for Tolstoy, to the conscious life of human beings. It produces the "cleavage of consciousness" that is constantly wavering between living-for-now and living-for-later, living here and living elsewhere.

In the cleavage of consciousness, reflection on what life is invariably turns to a reflection on what life is not, and a reflection on life invariably turns to a reflection on death. In its most rudimentary formulation, reflection of life and death cannot help but to be conceived of in temporal, and even chronological terms. Death not only marks the endpoint of life, but conditions it from within one's life—particularly those moments of life that entail an awareness of death. This sort of reflection is, for Tolstoy, unremarkable. What is more noteworthy is the way that reflection on life necessitates a certain symmetry. Just as reflection on life—on my life— entails reflection on a future time when I will no longer be alive, so am I led to reflect on a time before I was alive. Both temporalities—after my life and before my life—extend to infinity. And my life itself, suddenly constricted to a brief, ephemeral, and insignificant point, will have been nearly erased altogether by the weighty temporal shadows "before life" and "after life." My life strangely seems to vanish—or rather, becomes co-extensive with—the vast expanses of space and time that define it. Schopenhauer notes something along these lines when he comments that this time outside of life—*a parte post* and *a parte ante*—form a single, impersonal, indifferent continuity, with only "the intervention of an ephemeral life-dream" between them.[2]

The cleavage of consciousness, though it is preoccupied with the very human problems of my life, ends up producing a strange thought: that my life is not in fact my life. My life is personal, but this is because I've made it so, because it has been made so for me. But reflection on "before life" and "after life" reveals something *impersonal* about life. As Tolstoy notes, in reflecting on life in this way, "[r]easonable consciousness, imperceptibly developing in his personality, reaches a stage at which personal life becomes impossible" (Tolstoy, 45).

The impossibility of personal life: the point at which reflection on life renders life irreducible to either personal life or species life. The point at which the notion that life is reducible to my life or the life-for-us as a group or species becomes an untenable notion.

The cleavage of consciousness highlights the paradoxical nature of life when thought by human life in particular. The pinnacle of life is human life, which in turn renders life as a problem, in the form of contradictions (one life against another on which it depends; concrete instances of the living, in conflict with one another, juxtaposed to an abstract life that encompasses them). It invites us to name what we might call *Tolstoy's paradox*: For human beings, life is that which undermines itself in the process of revealing itself.

5.

But what would be the thought that would render such deeply-ingrained notions - my life, the life-for-us as human beings—as untenable? The very question indicates for Tolstoy the dawning of "reasonable consciousness." The phrase is misleading, appearing to indicate a facile reaffirmation of individual, human choice. But Tolstoy uses "reason" in counterintuitive ways. Reasonable consciousness is the awareness of the "cleavage of consciousness" (living now vs. living later), combined with the uncanny intuition of the "impossibility of personal life." Here "reason" is not simply a form of thought in service of the individual, personal, human subject— quite the reverse. Both the Pharisees and Scribes—religion and science—make this mistake. "In both cases the mistake arises from confusing personality—individuality, as science terms it—with the reasonable consciousness" (Tolstoy, 66).

Reasonable consciousness leads one towards an understanding of life as non-human—and as *fundamentally* non-human. It involves two aspects. One aspect relies on the philosophical notion of "sufficient reason": that there is an order in the external world itself that has some correlate, however dim, within the reasoning human mind. Another aspect is that reasonable consciousness is the product of the zooming-out effect, a scaling-up in which the reasoning human subject becomes aware of its contingency, aware that "life" is not reducible to the life-for-us as human beings, much less the life-for-me as a person.

For Tolstoy, reasonable consciousness entails a double refusal: a refusal of personality, of the ego, of psychology; and a refusal of the animal, of the organism, of biology. Reasonable consciousness is reflection on life that pulls apart life from human life, at the same time that the former absorbs the latter; the human life thinking life as non-human.

6.

What Tolstoy calls "reasonable consciousness" is not reason in the service of the human, even though it may be reason as the pinnacle of the human. Reasonable consciousness is not a blind leap of faith in a life after life of the Pharisees, but neither is it a reduction of life to the scientific and instrumental reason of the Scribes. Once one enters the space of reasonable consciousness, all notions of life—as human life—are questioned. All values that have highlighted and safeguarded life—religious or scientific—are suddenly thrown into abeyance. Reasonable consciousness is a reflection on life in which life is not reducible to human life, just as life-in-itself is not reducible to the life-for-us as human beings. "The discovery that human life is not merely personal existence—a truth humanity reached by thousands of years of spiritual toil—has become in the moral world a truth for man. . . a truth even more unquestionable and indestructible than the rotation of the earth and the law of gravitation" (Tolstoy, 86).

It is at this point that Tolstoy introduces what may be a surprising term: love. Love is, for Tolstoy, the only adequate response to the view of a non-human life given by reasonable consciousness. But the type of the love Tolstoy has in mind is as far from the brotherly love preached by religion as it is from procreation and reproduction as studied by science. Love is, for Tolstoy, defined by the selfless act, the giving of oneself over to an other, to the Other.

But this is, of course, easier said than done. Some interesting dilemmas are produced in the course of Tolstoy's discussion of love. For instance, Tolstoy begins to move away from the ethical notion of love when he notes that love is part and parcel of the contradiction of life. The love for one person may entail a hatred for another, and many gifts are not returned in kind. Tolstoy redefines love in more austere terms; he takes up the idea of selfless love and delimits it: "The possibility of true love begins only when man has understood that there is no welfare for his animal personality" (Tolstoy, 100). Love is rooted in a refusal, not only of selfishness, but of the self altogether. Tolstoy's language is reminiscent of that of the mystics: "Only when a man not only gives to another his time and strength, but wears out his body for the loved object and gives his life for it, do we all recognize that this is love" (Tolstoy, 104). Words like these one finds echos of Teresea of Avila or the ascetics of the hesychast tradition.

While there are echoes of this type of love in the history of religion and the wisdom traditions, the dilemma that Tolstoy has created is unique. If life is not reducible to human life, and if reasonable consciousness makes us aware that life is fundamentally non-human, then what would be the love adequate to such a life? As Tolstoy notes, "true love is life itself" (Tolstoy, 105). But if life is not human, and if the "true life" entails a dual refusal of the personality and the animal, then would not love also have to be non-human? Why, we might ask, should such an act of love be limited to the sphere of human ethical conduct? Beyond the love one feels for another human being, or indeed for the human itself, wouldn't there also be another love, a love for the non-human? In this sense love is the act of giving oneself over to this non-human life.

7.

Without directly resolving this dilemma, Tolstoy does evoke a type of love most often associated with mystical traditions, that of *agape*: a divine love that is unconditional and self-sacrificing. But Tolstoy rarely evokes a monotheistic God or savior that would serve as a model for such a divine love, much less a chosen group of the faithful for whom such a sacrifice would be made. If Tolstoy's evocation of love takes place within a non-human life, then towards whom or what is this love directed? One thinks of Augustine's famous refrain in the *Confessions*: Whom do I love when I love God?[3]

It is here that Tolstoy discusses suffering. Certainly there are forms of suffering that have discernible causes and for which accountability can be made. An action produces a reaction, a cause necessitates an effect. But many forms of suffering appear to have no discernible cause at all, and they must be suffered without meaning or moral. These latter are the sufferings of the mystics, though the sense of their inexplicability is not limited to religion or the saints. It is a basic feature of the modern, pessimistic outlook, caught between a life forever deferred by the Pharisees and interminably measured by the Scribes.

Tolstoy finds that, stark as it may be, suffering actually reveals something noteworthy, and that is the non-human aspect of life, the life that is indifferent to us, the *impersonal* life, concisely put in the title to the thirty-fourth chapter of his essay: "The inexplicability of the sufferings of earthly existence proves to man more convincingly than anything else that his life is not the life of the personality which begins at birth and ends at death" (Tolstoy, 145). Paradoxically, for Tolstoy suffering actually reveals life—not just the misery of human life, but impersonal life, the life at once indifferent to but inseparable from human life. Tolstoy seems to be suggesting here that "true life" is the awareness of non-human life via human living, expressed at its most poignant in our dark durations of inexplicable and senseless suffering.

A strange eternity emerges from this: "To believe in the destruction of life because the body is destroyed, is the same as to believe that the disappearance of the shadow of an object when the object merges into full light, is a proof of the destruction of the object itself" (Tolstoy, 128).

(Notes)

1 This dichotomy between "Life" and "the living" is the basis for my book, Eugene Thacker, *After Life*.
2 See Schopenhauer, 2:467.
3 See Augustine, book X, chap. VI, 87ff.

Works Cited:

Augustine. *Confessions*. Tr. William Watts. Cambridge, MA: Harvard UP, 2000

Thacker, Eugene. *After Life*. Chicago: University of Chicago Press, 2010

Tolstoy, Leo. *On Life and Essays on Religion*. Tr. Aylmer Maude. Oxford: Oxford UP, 1934

Schopenhauer, Arthur. *The World as Will and Representation*. Tr. E. F. J. Payne. 2 vols. New York: Dover, 1960

Contributors

Michael D. Gordin is Rosengarten Professor of Modern and Contemporary History at Princeton University, where he specializes in the history of modern science. He is the author of five monographs, including *A Well-Ordered Thing: Dmitrii Mendeleev and the Shadow of the Periodic Table* (Basic Books, 2004) and *Scientific Babel: How Science Was Done before and after Global English* (2015), as well as a series of articles on the cultural history of Russian and Soviet science.

Jeff Love is Research Professor of German and Russian at Clemson University. He has published two books on Tolstoy, *The Overcoming of History in War and Peace* (Brill, 2004) and *Tolstoy: A Guide for the Perplexed* (Continuum, 2008). He is also co-translator of Schelling's *Philosophical Investigations into the Essence of Human Freedom* (State University of New York Press, 2006), co-editor of *Nietzsche and Dostoevsky: Philosophy, Morality, Tragedy* (Northwestern, 2016) and editor of *Heidegger in Russia and Eastern Europe* (Rowman & Littlefield, 2017). His most recent book is *The Black Circle: A Life of Alexandre Kojève* (Columbia, 2018).

Inessa Medzhibovskaya is an Associate Professor of Liberal Studies and Literature at the New School for Social Research and Lang College in New York City. She is the author of *Tolstoy and the Religious Culture of His Time* (Lexington/Rowman and Littlefield, 2008, paperback 2009) and of *Tolstoy's On Life (from the Archival History of Russian Philosophy)* (the Tolstoy Society of North America, 2019), and of over fifty essays and book chapters on Russian authors and philosophers, ideology and education, and the interplay of philosophy, religion, politics and literary aesthetics. She has recently edited a critical edition of Tolstoy's *On Life* co-translated with Michael Denner (Northwestern,

2018) and *Tolstoy and His Problems: Views from the Twenty-First Century* (Northwestern, 2018). In addition to a new monograph, *Tolstoy ad the Fates of the Twentieth Century* (for Princeton), she is working to complete the first anthology of Tolstoy's thought in English, and a companion volume of introduction to his thought (forthcoming from Academic Studies Press).

Randall A. Poole is Professor of History at the College of St. Scholastica in Duluth, Minnesota. His research areas include Russian and European intellectual history, the history of ideas, and the history of philosophical and religious thought. He is a Fellow of the Center for the Study of Law and Religion at Emory University in Atlanta, Georgia, and a Fellow of the International Center for the Study of Russian Philosophy at the Institute of Philosophy, Saint Petersburg State University. In 2012 he was Visiting Professor of Russian Intellectual History at the University of Toronto. He is the translator and editor of *Problems of Idealism: Essays in Russian Social Philosophy* (Yale University Press, 2003); co-editor (with G. M. Hamburg) of *A History of Russian Philosophy, 1830-1930: Faith, Reason, and the Defense of Human Dignity* (Cambridge University Press, 2010, 2013); and co-editor (with Paul W. Werth) of *Religious Freedom in Modern Russia* (University of Pittsburgh Press, 2018). He is also the author of numerous articles and book chapters.

James A. Scanlan (1927-2016) was Emeritus Professor of Philosophy at The Ohio State University. He was a specialist in the history of Russian philosophical thought, both literary and nonliterary, with emphasis on the nineteenth century, especially the thought of Dostoevsky and Tolstoy. He authored and edited many books, including *Marxism in the USSR: A Critical Survey of Current Soviet Thought* (Cornell, 1985); *Technology, Culture, and Development: the Experience of the Soviet Model* (M.E. Sharpe, 1992); *Russian Thought After Communism: the Recovery of a Philosophical Heritage* (M.E. Sharpe, 1994); and *Dostoevsky the Thinker* (Cornell, 2002). He was also a co-editor of three volumes of *Russian Philosophy* (1965), an essential anthology of Russian thought, and translated and edited Mikhail Gershenzon's *A History of Young Russia* (Charles Schlacks, 1986).

Eugene Thacker is author of several books, including In *The Dust of This Planet* (Zero Books, 2011) and *After Life* (University of Chicago Press, 2010). His most recent book is *Infinite Resignation* (Repeater, 2019). He is Professor of Culture and Media at The New School in New York City.

Index